Hawthorne's
Tragic Vision

Hawthorne's
Tragic Vision

By Roy R. Male

Austin
University of Texas Press

Library of Congress Catalog Card No. 57–7560
© 1957 by the University of Texas Press

Manufactured in the United States of America
by the Printing Division of the University of Texas

To Carolyn

Preface

READERS familiar with Nathaniel Hawthorne's fiction will not be greatly surprised to learn that his view of life was essentially tragic. But it seems to me that the details of that vision and the organic relation of his major works have not yet been fully perceived. Hence this book.

In writing it, I have incurred numerous pleasant obligations. My indebtedness to previous Hawthorne scholarship will be apparent in the footnotes, but I may single out here the biographical and editorial work of Randall Stewart, Norman Holmes Pearson, and Newton Arvin, and the sensitive criticism of the late F. O. Matthiessen and of Richard Harter Fogle and Hyatt Howe Waggoner. Randall Stewart and Victor A. Elconin read the entire manuscript, and Stanley K. Coffman offered helpful criticism of Chapter VI. I have profited considerably from conversa-

PREFACE

tions with a group of perceptive students at the University of Oklahoma, including Hillel Chodos, Thomas Huckaby, John L. Murphy, and Dan Wheeler.

Most of Chapter IV and parts of Chapter VIII first appeared in *The Publications of the Modern Language Association* and in *College English*, respectively; I am indebted to the editors of those journals for permission to reprint. The Faculty Research Committee at the University of Oklahoma and Melvin W. Askew have been very helpful in typing the manuscript. Finally, I am indebted to the Brooks Foundation for aid in its publication.

ROY R. MALE

Norman, Oklahoma
December, 1956

Contents

Hawthorne's
Tragic Vision

A time to rend, and a time to sew.
Ecclesiastes 3:7

i ~

Introduction

FROM ITS BEGINNING, America has been a predominantly masculine venture: an experi-
ment in religious protest, a speculative development of real
estate, a gamble that movement westward might assure not
only prosperity but also some kind of moral purification. As
new fields have been conquered, the instruments for converting matter and energy into useful forms have multiplied:
condensers, converters, transformers, dynamos, and now
transistors and reactors. It need hardly be said that all this
physical transformation has occurred without any noticeable
change in the problem of moral growth—except, perhaps, to
distract us from its central importance.

The predominance of a spatial and speculative vision in this country has continually produced various efforts to achieve rebirth without roots and Christianity without the crucifixion. By temperament Thomas Paine was an American, and his views on this subject, though stamped by his own brand of eighteenth-century deism and stated too bluntly for most American tastes, provide a striking illustration. Urging in *The Age of Reason* that God should be studied in the scripture of creation rather than in the Bible, Paine concluded that the true theology is natural science, especially astronomy. "I recollect not a single passage in all the writings ascribed to the men called apostles," he said, "that conveys any idea of what God is. These writings are chiefly controversial, and the gloominess of the subject they dwell upon, that of a man dying in agony on a cross, is better suited to the gloomy genius of a monk in a cell, by whom it was not impossible they were written, than to any man breathing the open air of the Creation."[1] Few Americans would have pressed as far toward agnosticism as Paine did. But his utter failure to comprehend the meaning of the Christian tragedy and his appeal to "the open air" have recurred in various forms, from Emerson's plea for "men drenched in time to recover themselves and taste their native immortal air" to twentieth-century versions of Christ as supersalesman and positive thinker.

In this predominantly masculine enterprise, the role of woman has always been anomalous. The notorious ineptitude of the heroine in Western films serves as a constant reminder that in a world of movement in space, a woman was simply an encumbrance. Her alternatives were to remain behind in

[1] *The Life and Works of Thomas Paine,* ed. William M. Van der Weyde (Thomas Paine Historical Association, New Rochelle, N.Y., 1925), VIII, 48.

Introduction

the ancestral homestead or to adapt herself to man's ways in the covered wagon and the squatter's hut. Without density and intrigue, there was no action possible for her in fiction except the monotonous paling and blushing that we associate with Cooper's refined heroines, the grim endurance of mannish Esther Bush in *The Prairie*, or the flamboyant marksmanship of Hurricane Nell in the dime novels. Before *The Scarlet Letter* no American writer understood the values of time, tragedy, or womanhood well enough to create a woman in fiction.

Hawthorne's grasp of these values was not abstract; he understood them in his medium, which was the romance. His well-known distinction between the romance and the novel no longer possesses much critical significance, since the modern novel has assumed the "latitude, both as to its fashion and material" that Hawthorne reserved for the romance. But a proper appreciation of Hawthorne's work depends upon a knowledge of his medium. To be comprehensive, a definition of Hawthorne's romance should be based not only on his explicit statements in the prefaces but also on his practice. Originally, the romance was a work written in the vernacular, a medium not so far removed from Hawthorne's as might at first appear. He sought a realm where the "actual and the imaginary" might meet, a way of expressing "the highest truths through the humblest medium of familiar words and images" (V, 173).[2] What this amounts to in his accomplished work is a rare combination of poetry and fiction: poetry, in that each image functions as part of a larger design; fiction,

[2] All citations to Hawthorne's writings refer to *The Works of Nathaniel Hawthorne*, ed. George P. Lathrop (Houghton Mifflin Company, Boston, 1882–83), 13 vols. Citations to volume and page of this edition are given in parentheses when the reader might have some difficulty finding the quotation. Italics in passages quoted from Hawthorne are mine unless otherwise indicated.

in that the narrative is woven in a "humble texture" that preserves some degree of verisimilitude.

Hawthorne's insistence upon functional imagery accounts in part for his popularity today. The modern critical tendency toward reading fiction as poetry, emphasizing image, symbol, and allegory, often results in distortion when it is applied to novels like *The Red Badge of Courage*.[3] But Hawthorne's fiction lights up when examined under this kind of intensive scrutiny. Sophia Hawthorne once remarked that her husband was "extremely scrupulous about the value and effect of every expression" (VII, 413); his conscious artistry, though doubtless often tacitly appreciated in the past, has only in recent years been explicitly recognized. Hawthorne knew very well the limitations of his narrative talent; he never fully appreciated his genius as a poet.

But his real strength will never be revealed by criticism that insists solely upon image-counting or study of fictional techniques. Hawthorne possessed what one of his friends called "the awful power of insight," and his fiction remains valuable chiefly because of its penetration into the essential truths of the human heart. His one fruitful subject was the problem of moral growth. This limitation was also a great virtue, for it kept his mind free from the sort of irrelevant clutter that contaminated Poe's fiction and much of Whitman's poetry. When his moral imagination was not engaged, Hawthorne wrote things like "Little Daffydowndilly" and "David Swan"; when it was, even in a mere sketch like "Fancy's Show Box," he is always worth reading.

To the traditional definition of the romance as a love story Hawthorne added a dignity that stemmed from his deep understanding of the relation between man and woman,

[3] See Philip Rahv, "Fiction and the Criticism of Fiction," *Kenyon Review*, XVIII (Spring, 1956), 276–99.

7

IntroductionIntroduction

space and time, comedy and tragedy. Each of his major romances *is* a love story in a sense that may be explained by summing up his view of the rhythms in human experience. Originally, the young man lives in a world where the surname is irrelevant or blotted out. He is Robin in "My Kinsman, Major Molineux," or Donatello in *The Marble Faun*, acting without understanding his actions, chiefly concerned with new particulars and not much interested in their relationships. Like the young Oedipus, his "outsight" is excellent but his insight is extremely limited. He penetrates into space and is a master of locomotion; the undisciplined dance of gesture and attitude is his natural mode of expression. He keeps playing new roles, wearing new uniforms, hoping to find one that will fit his inner self. In short, his angle of vision is essentially protestant, revolutionary, and spatial; when fully informed, it is an attitude that is crucially important for changing men's minds.

This ability to speculate, to rend old patterns, is the prerogative of the man. Normally, his maturity comes through the shocks of love and marriage. For the woman's natural role is to conserve and clothe in time. While she shares some of youth's irresponsibility, as potential childbearer she is automatically linked to time. She needs the man to provide her escape from the ancestral homestead; he needs her to keep him from aimless movement in space. To the man she offers an ambiguous promise of involvement and redemption, passion and purification. If the man will accept her, not deceived or stunned by this ambiguity, he may go on to higher insights, as Dimmesdale does in *The Scarlet Letter*.

For terms that will be broad enough to describe these masculine and feminine values, I have taken a cue from Kenneth Burke and chosen two words from the vocabulary of finance: "speculation" and "investment." Ordinarily used as monetary terms, they carry over into other fields. Under "speculation" I include the activities implied by Solomon's statement that there is "a time to rend." "Speculation" is the business of the head;[4] it is man's prerogative of gambling on something new, of experimenting, of penetrating into space, sparked by Promethean fire. "Investment" is the abstract equivalent of Solomon's counterbalancing statement that there is "a time to sew." It is the function of the heart, the feminine role of conserving and clothing in time. These terms help to reveal the irony with which Hawthorne viewed the frequent efforts to substitute rapid technological change and industrial wealth for moral progress, an irony most clearly illustrated in "The Celestial Railroad."

As "love stories," Hawthorne's romances are centered upon the Original Sin. For it seems clear that he interpreted the Original Sin as the mutual love of man and woman. The most explicit evidence for this view is to be found in "The Maypole of Merry Mount." Edith and Edgar (their jarring, fluffy names are a sign of the tale's early composition) discover that "from the moment that they truly loved, they had subjected themselves to earth's doom of care and sorrow, and troubled joy, and had no more a home at Merry Mount. That was Edith's mystery." This simple statement is expanded, tested, and reiterated in later works, from *The Scarlet Letter* to *The Marble Faun*. The union of man and woman depends upon a rending of their original relation to the parent and upon a partial inversion of their natural roles. The woman

[4] In a letter to Sophia dated April 6, 1840, Hawthorne wrote: "Hearts never do understand the mystery of separation—that is the business of the head." (Quotations from Hawthorne's letters to Sophia are from the originals in the Huntington Library and are quoted by permission of its director, John E. Pomfret. Randall Stewart and Norman Holmes Pearson, who are editing Hawthorne's letters, have also kindly permitted me to quote these passages.)

Introduction

must become curious about man's province of knowledge; the man must become passionately attracted to the woman and through this attraction become involved with time, sin, and suffering. The fruit of their union will be, like Pearl, at once a token of sin and a promise of redemption.

Some suspicion that the love of man and woman was the Original Sin has always been latent, it seems, in theology. It can be inferred from Paul's highly ambiguous remarks about marriage in his First Epistle to the Corinthians, and it appears in Augustine's tortured wrestling with the problem of conjugal union before the Fall in Book XIV of *The City of God*. But if Hawthorne derived this rather unorthodox interpretation from any source, it was doubtless from *Paradise Lost*, though Milton's discursive pronouncements in the *Treatise of Christian Doctrines* give it no support. The idea has the advantage of clarifying several riddles. It immediately explains how all mankind sinned in Adam's Fall, since all were offspring of the sin; it illuminates the prophecy that Eve's seed would bruise the head of the serpent, and also the virgin birth of Christ. But the temporal interval between the sin and the redemption, Adam's crime and Christ's atonement, is crucially important. If obliterated, it leads to the fallacious formula of the Fortunate Fall. Hawthorne believed that moral growth cannot occur without sin and suffering; he never accepted the glib converse of this proposition, that sin is automatically redemptive.

The original tragic action may thus be described as a threefold movement: first the parental bond is established; it is broken as the individual proudly asserts his independence from the father and accepts a new bondage to his mate; and finally, after the terrible human cost of sin, agony, and death, some degree of spiritual purification and re-establishment of the original bond is achieved. The sin is a form of adultery,

HAWTHORNE'S TRAGIC VISION

a "commixture," as Hawthorne calls it, in which one set of values is merged with another so that the original functions of the individual are partially inverted. Thus Eve speculates, experiments, and is seduced by her curiosity concerning man's knowledge, while Adam is overcome by the "sinister rib" of female charm. The part of the woman or her surrogate in this action is obviously central. The young man approaches her as a more or less one-dimensional figure. But she is dual: sinner and saint, earthly and heavenly. The vessel containing both poison and possible redemption, she presents a baffling ambiguity of evil and good.[5]

Hawthorne's best stories are all concerned in one way or another with this central situation. If we dismiss *Fanshawe*, which he correctly considered immature, and the late frag- mentary romances, which, despite Edward H. Davidson's heroic editorial work, remain too incomplete for satisfactory analysis, we are left with about eight or nine short stories of permanent value and the four major romances. The other short tales and sketches possess considerable biographical interest and offer many clues for interpreting Hawthorne's perfectly achieved works. But we do his art no service by placing too much emphasis upon them.

Four early stories, "The Maypole of Merry Mount," "The Gentle Boy," "Roger Malvin's Burial," and "My Kinsman, Major Molineux," are concerned with the quest for a home, the search for a parent. As will be pointed out in Chapter III, the search for a home in America has consistently been a

[5] This duality is a recurring theme in Hawthorne's letters written to Sophia during their courtship. For him, Sophia was both the dark and the light woman. "My wayward heart," he wrote on January 25, 1840, "will love this naughty Sophie Hawthorne; yes, its affection for the Dove is doubled, because she is inseparably united with naughty Sophie. I have one love for them both, and it is infinitely intensified because they share it together."

Introduction

physical manifestation of a psychological and spiritual pilgrimage, directed toward finding an identity and an integrated religious experience. The characteristic youthful ideal of a home without roots—a tent on a raft floating down the Mississippi, a massive convertible, a ship or its inland counterpart, the covered wagon—might be paralleled by our typical foreign policy, in which after years of avoiding "entanglements" with the dark ambiguities of the East we have at last been confronted by the necessity of knowing foreign countries in their full temporal context. We still seek to gain by incessant motion what we have lost in space and never knew in time, but the inadequacy of this endless shuttling is now much more apparent.

Chapter IV is a discussion of "Rappaccini's Daughter," a complex story that directly anticipates *The Scarlet Letter.* Here, in the "Eden of the present world," is the first of Hawthorne's dark women: exotic, dual, and fascinating. The young man, Giovanni Guasconti, misses his opportunity for moral growth. Baffled by the ambiguity of the good and evil he finds in Beatrice, he tries to separate the physical attraction from the pure ideal and eventually accepts the mundane Baglioni's proposal of bringing her within "the limits of ordinary nature," making it merely an amorous adventure.

All mankind comes into the world with the birthmark of the Original Sin. But there are various ways of avoiding its repetition. One may try to transform the duality of woman into something simple and pure, as Aylmer does in "The Birthmark." One may wed his art instead of the woman, as Warland does in "The Artist of the Beautiful." But in the effort to avoid the Original Sin, man may discover something worse. In seeking ultimate penetration, Ethan Brand inverts his vision, ruthlessly uses the woman as a mere experiment in evil, and follows his satanic prototype in committing the aboriginal, the unpardonable, sin. Thus there is no efficient antidote for the shocks of recognition that assail Young Goodman Brown, who, like Giovanni Guasconti, is stupefied by the ambiguity of good and evil he discovers in his Faith. There is no smooth detour to the celestial city.

In the profound symmetrical structure of *The Scarlet Letter* we see the given elements of the moral situation. There is the woman, wedded to guilt yet offering eventual beatitude to the man if they will both accept, undeceived, her tragic promise and find the "oneness of their being" in Pearl. There is the man, involved through his passion with woman and thus with guilt—involved, that is, with life and the inexorable flow of time. So long as he avoids full commitment, his grip upon the intellectual tradition is encased in a false glove; he preaches the word, but it is hollow, without the vision, the life. And there are two masterly personifications: Pearl, the precocious offspring of the sin and thus the visible embodiment of the inscrutable truth, and Roger Chillingworth, the image of guilt.

In *The Scarlet Letter* we see that to develop one's human potential one must plunge into the pit in order to ascend. To ascend the platform with Hester is to suffer the wounds, to become involved with life and art, to sew the threads of social responsibility. But there is also a time to rend. To ascend with Dimmesdale is to break down the walls, to discard the hollow glove, the old notes, the outward forms. It is to find a point of view in which the past really enlivens and illuminates the present. And it is to discover that the truth cannot be grasped abstractly, that the process of knowing is ultimately consummated in art and in the artistically structured life.

In Hawthorne's fiction, the union of man and woman is both a fact and a trope representing the dialectic between present and past, rebellion and acceptance, space and time. There is no dark woman in *The House of the Seven Gables;* her ambiguous qualities are symbolized in the house itself, while the masculine qualities are represented by the inhabitants of the street. The house is a veritable "womb of time." Hawthorne anticipates Bergson's distinction between duration—the interpenetration of past, present, and future as we know it in immediate experience—and abstract or clock time —the scientific, spatial measurement of discrete instants. Duration is exemplified in the house, where the shades of the past merge with the present like the notes of a melody; abstract time is illustrated by Judge Pyncheon's undeviating chronometer. The high points of the book occur when the inhabitants of one realm invade the alien but attractive opposite.

The Blithedale Romance is Hawthorne's dark comedy. The detachment of comedy, he felt, was necessary for changing men's minds; the involvement of tragedy, however, was necessary for changing their hearts. The Blithedale experiment typified the belief that the tragic rhythm of the seasons could be obliterated, that winter could be converted into May through intellectual effort and withdrawal to new lands. Zenobia attempts to avoid the tragic implications of womanhood; Hollingsworth erects an intellectual shield to protect him from passion; Coverdale remains an observer. Here again, the woman is linked to guilty knowledge, though this time it is the new knowledge of the Western world; here again in Priscilla is a "medium" of truth. But unlike Hester Prynne and Arthur Dimmesdale, Zenobia and Hollingsworth succeed in evading the Original Sin, only to commit an abortive form of it in the end. *The Blithedale Romance* is Hawthorne's most pessimistic book, and it is pessimistic because the characters attain no tragic understanding.

14

In *The Marble Faun* Hawthorne poses for the last time the question of transfiguration in life and in art. In *The Scarlet Letter* the man and woman were presented after the Fall; here we see the young man in all his timeless freedom as he collides with the woman who is already fallen. Linked to the very "model" of guilt but also closely bound to the prototype of redemption, Miriam is like Rome in being the vessel of all time.[6] Hilda, as the spiritual ideal, is both personification and character, and this, we shall discover, is one of the difficulties in the book. But its shortcomings need not detain us here. For *The Marble Faun* casts a grand light back over all of Hawthorne's work and confirms the point we have been making—that his tragic vision in the romances eventually leads back through *Paradise Lost* to Ecclesiastes and Genesis.

As this summary indicates, one of my assumptions in examining the major romances is that the allegorical personifications are valuable chiefly for the way they illumine the action of the principal characters. They are not simple personifications like Patience and Charity; they possess enough complexity to be interesting in their own right. But to ignore their allegorical function is to miss part of Hawthorne's charm. He was also a symbolic writer, and the usual sharp distinction between symbolism and allegory is not much help in interpreting his fiction. The scarlet letter, for example, finally becomes nearly as multivalent as the white whale in *Moby Dick*. As I attempt to show in the following chapter, Hawthorne shared the belief of Emerson and other contem-

[6] Here and elsewhere I am indebted to R. W. B. Lewis, *The American Adam: Innocence, Tragedy, and Tradition in the Nineteenth Century* (University of Chicago Press, Chicago, 1955, hereafter cited as *The American Adam*), for his extremely suggestive description of "a native American mythology" and for his orientation of *The Marble Faun* in this larger pattern.

poraries that art should develop from within. But to the expansive, somewhat shapeless tendencies inherent in the Emersonian version of the organic principle, Hawthorne opposed a rare and beautiful sense of form, of the generic as a condition in art as in life.

This balance, the profound symmetry of his work, is not merely a matter of technique. It expresses the tempered steel of the man and the artist, his ability to grasp the riddle of the Sphinx unflinchingly and humanely. Man does keep his balance by maturing in three phases, the fateful triple crossroads of *Oedipus Rex*. His "four-legged" faunlike stance, the youthful self, is released chiefly through an act of will. Partially severing the parental bond, he discovers his identity in a group. (For a potential author, of course, this group may be writers in a particular literary tradition; he comes to know Spenser and Milton, say, as the usual college student knows his fraternity brothers.) As a result of this identification he creates a sort of magic royalty for himself; life is an Eden, a circus, a carnival. Nothing can touch him: the prophecy, the ghost, the Original Sin are buried behind him; the past and the future do not impinge upon the present.

Two interwoven patterns of failure to achieve this initial transformation may be discerned in American culture. The first, prevalent in New England two centuries ago, occurs when the parents impose too heavy a burden from the past upon the children. Unable to break away from the ancestral structure, these "time-drenched" youths (the term is Emerson's, and he was one of them) miss the initiation or come to it too late. Hawthorne's unforgettable portrait of this type is Clifford Pyncheon, and it is no accident that Clifford spouts a wild parody of Emersonian doctrine when he finally escapes from his bondage to the past. As Hawthorne interpreted New

England's history, the great crime of the first generation of Puritans consisted in their rigid imposition of an essentially sound but aged view of life upon their children.

Little need be said about the other pattern of failure, which exactly reverses this situation. In our literature and our lives we are all too familiar with youths who have nothing to react against. Unpruned and unweeded, these spiritual orphans blunder from one meaningless episode and group to another, wandering in a desperate, soupy fog. An orphan himself, but also beset by an oppressive past, Hawthorne was fortunate in knowing the pressure of these aberrations and still more fortunate in being able to avoid them. With the aid of his uncle, he found an appropriately youthful identity at Bowdoin; with his native gifts he found a literary identity in the tradition of Spenser, Milton, and Bunyan.

The second transformation Hawthorne postponed, perhaps because, as his love letters to Sophia Peabody indicate, he saw its implications more clearly than most young men. To stand on two legs, the youth must sacrifice the Eden he has discovered. Indeed, the very qualities that may have made him conspicuously successful in the morning of his life—good looks, ease of movement—will, if unchanged, weaken and warp him in middle age. This conversion is literally a "turning together"; it is crucial, a crux, a crossroad; and it cannot be achieved by an act of will or by intellectual effort alone. As the woman moves from a relatively passive state to an active one, the man is impelled by passion. Transformation occurs only when action and passion, head and heart are fused in the fiery crucible. Hawthorne pictures the vessels of purification—the elixir, the woman, the heart, and the fire—as ambiguous agents of destruction and creation. The heart is a foul cavern; but for the man it is the source of life, the great converter.

American fiction is rich in examples of youths who fail to be transformed. Amasa Delano in Melville's "Benito Cereno" and Anson Hunter in Fitzgerald's "The Rich Boy" come immediately to mind. More impressive are men like Ahab and Ethan Brand, who try to achieve conversion on a grand scale by the sheer force of an unchastened will, the hollowness of their hearts matched by the swelling of their rhetoric, the fiery crucible locked inside their being. Hawthorne's imagination was also engaged by the frightening possibility that passion may so overwhelm a man that he becomes welded to a vision of evil, like young Goodman Brown, or enfeebled in will, like Arthur Dimmesdale at the beginning of *The Scarlet Letter*.

The triadic stance, the perception gained in the evening of man's life, grows out of the action of his youth and the passion that ushered in his maturity. It is exactly the opposite of the first phase, except that it also depends upon an act of will. Then he needs the group to find himself; now he must detach himself from it in order to confront his own soul. Only then does he see that the very sins and aberrations that separate him from others are the one universal bond of humanity. This, I take it, is the point of "The Minister's Black Veil." The Reverend Mr. Hooper arrives at this perception too early in his life, but it is entirely appropriate for his deathbed. A richer illustration of the rhythm of life is found at the end of *The Scarlet Letter,* where we see the man whose insights have been refined by his passion and strengthened by a newly discovered will, the child who has become humanized, and the woman who endures.

In Hawthorne's view, it is inevitable that at any given stage of life man will be somewhat askew and that he will be confronted by ambiguity and paradox. How can he rebel and accept, improvise a sermon and participate in an age-old ritual, speculate and invest at the same time? He can do so only at certain crucial moments of revelation—those epiphanies when transformation occurs. These, of course, are the high points of Hawthorne's fiction: the *Walpurgisnacht* in "Young Goodman Brown," the forest and pillory scenes in *The Scarlet Letter*, the escape of Clifford and Hepzibah from the House of the Seven Gables, the carnival in *The Marble Faun*.

Much of our difficulty in understanding Hawthorne comes from an effort to state his ideas in abstract, static form. When we do so fairly, we arrive at the unresolved "doubleness" noted by several critics, in which Hawthorne is seen as a Protestant who yearned to be a Catholic, a defender of Puritanism who satirized his ancestors, a Romantic who attacked Transcendentalism, a skeptic and a believer, and so on. But when a man's life is stretched out in time, when the narrative rhythm is preserved, there is no lack of resolution and no ambiguity except the final mystery, namely that the full turning of the wheel and the complete perception come only as man's life ends. Donatello, for example, moves from the morning to the afternoon of his life; Dimmesdale, from the afternoon to the evening. As Hawthorne's very style indicates, each step is fraught with alternative possibilities; but the way itself is perfectly clear. Man solves the riddle of the Sphinx by moving from action through passion to perception, a cycle that leads up to his death. He may attempt to avoid this tragic rhythm, but if he does so he is consumed, like Ethan Brand, too soon.

We need to keep these universal conditions of moral growth in mind to prevent confusion in reading Hawthorne. Any reader who approaches his work with the vague notion that these stories are simply concerned with the effects of sin, as the cliché goes, will never fully appreciate Hawthorne's art. But naked Everyman is dull. Once the unity of Hawthorne's art is established, its variety can be better appre-

Introduction

ciated. He complicated and intensified the problems of conversion by every means at his command; he tested just about every possible alternative to the union between man and woman; he experimented with such techniques as first-person narration; he found a different metaphor for each book. My aim will be to preserve a sense of this variety while at the same time I try to indicate the unified design of his work.

The youthful will probably always consider tragedy "gloomy" and "morbid." Hawthorne must have heard this judgment of his work so often that he half-believed it to be true. The young like to keep past, present, and future in separate compartments; the complex intertwining simply confuses and unnerves them, as it did young Goodman Brown. It takes time to realize that the final mood of Hawthorne's tragedy is a tempered hopefulness, a realization that out of sin, sorrow, and decay may be born the insights, the "words of flame" uttered by Arthur Dimmesdale in the Election Sermon.

Hawthorne was not a great novelist, in the strict sense of that term. His grasp of the actual surface of life was firm but quite limited in comparison to Dickens or Stendhal or Balzac. But, as he kept insisting, Hawthorne was a romancer. He *did* merge poetry and fiction, the imaginary and the actual, the universal and the particular. He stands midway between Dickens and Edwin Arlington Robinson in a realm of his own. Once we grasp his meanings in this unusual yet conventional medium, we recognize his absolute greatness as a writer and the centrality of his position in American literature.

ii ~

The Organic-Mechanical Antithesis

THE ROMANTIC CONCEPTION of the universe as organic and dynamic may be described as one of the two fundamental ideas Emerson, Thoreau, Hawthorne, Melville, and Whitman held in common, the other being their faith in democracy. They differed markedly, of course, as individual writers. Furthermore, Hawthorne and Melville interpreted the ethical implications of the organic metaphor so that it led back to Solomon's tragic wisdom about the seasons rather than to Emerson's *Nature*. But they all agreed that the full complexity of human life is best approached through metaphor, symbol, and myth; that mechanical, mathematical, and static concepts are incapable of

The Organic-Mechanical Antithesis

grasping the rhythmic unity of living things; and that man and his artistic achievements must be considered as an integral part of this unity. Emerson being moved by "strange sympathies" as he visited the Jardin des Plantes; Thoreau seeing himself among the pine trees or the lichens; Hawthorne suggesting that art, like nature, should develop from "the innermost germ"; Melville watching *Moby Dick* grow from within like branches on a tree; Whitman attempting to encompass his sprawling growth within the covers of *Leaves of Grass*—for these writers the organic metaphor expressed a fundamental attitude toward life and art.[1]

The exact sources of this idea cannot be determined with any certainty, since the organic doctrine had been promulgated by enough influential German and English writers to make it a part of the intellectual climate in Emerson's era. Yet it is clear that the thought of Goethe and the German Romanticists, as communicated to America chiefly through Coleridge and Carlyle, was the fountainhead of organic

[1] As I use it, the ambiguous but unavoidable term *Romantic* is to be taken as virtually synonymous with *organic*. Dissension about the adequacy of this definition will doubtless continue, but from a pragmatic point of view it seems well established. It is supported by an ever increasing body of scholarship. See Oskar Walzel, *German Romanticism*, trans. A. E. Lussky (G. P. Putnam's Sons, New York, 1932), pp. 61–70; Arthur O. Lovejoy, *The Great Chain of Being* (Harvard University Press, Cambridge, Mass., 1936), Chap. X; Alexander Gode-von Aesch, *Natural Science in German Romanticism* (Columbia University Press, New York, 1941), Chap. IV; Howard Mumford Jones, *Ideas in America* (Harvard University Press, Cambridge, Mass., 1945), pp. 134–36; Morse Peckham, "Towards a Theory of Romanticism," *Publications of the Modern Language Association*, LXVI (March, 1951), 5–23; R. P. Adams, "Romanticism and the American Renaissance," *American Literature*, XXIII (January, 1952), 419–32; Meyer H. Abrams, *The Mirror and the Lamp* (Oxford University Press, New York, 1953), Chap. VII; and Richard H. Fogle, "Organic Form in American Criticism, 1840–1870," in *The Development of American Literary Criticism*, ed. Floyd Stovall (University of North Carolina Press, Chapel Hill, N.C., 1955), pp. 75–111.

theory in this country. In his essay "Thomas Carlyle and His Works," Thoreau wrote that Carlyle's "earlier essays reached us at a time when Coleridge's were the only recent words which had made any notable impression so far." One of these "earlier essays," and undoubtedly a key text in the transmission of the new idea, was Carlyle's "Signs of the Times," which appeared in the *Edinburgh Review* in June, 1829. Although the article was anonymous, readers in New England soon realized that there was "a new power coming up in the literary republic," a power calling to arms those who were dissatisfied with the status quo.[2] The contemporary appeal of Carlyle's essay resulted chiefly from his vivid dichotomy between the mechanical and the organic:

Were we required to characterize this age of ours by any single epithet, we should be tempted to call it, not an Heroical, Devotional, Philosophical, or Moral Age, but, above all others, the Mechanical Age. It is the Age of Machinery, in every outward and inward sense of that word; the age which, with its whole undivided might, forwards, teaches and practices the great art of adapting means to ends.

Surveying the religion, science, literature, and government of his time, Carlyle found mechanism everywhere. In religion it seemed to him that "the Bible-society, professing a far higher and heavenly structure, is found on inquiry to be altogether an earthly contrivance: supported by collection of moneys, by fomenting of vanities, by puffing, intrigue, and

[2] Perry Miller, ed., *The Transcendentalists* (Harvard University Press, Cambridge, Mass., 1950), p. 39. In *The Dial*, II (July, 1841), 131, appeared this notice: "Although the name of Thomas Carlyle is rarely mentioned in the critical journals of this country, there is no living writer who is more sure of immediate attention from a large circle of readers or who exercises a greater influence than he in these United States. Since the publication of his article on the characteristics of our time in the *Edinburgh Review,* and afterwards of the *Sartor,* this influence has been deepening and extending year by year."

chicane; a machine for converting the heathen." Philosophy and psychology since Locke he characterized as materialistic and barren in all countries except Germany. "Hartley's vibrations and vibratiuncles, one would think, were material and mechanical enough; but our Continental neighbors have gone still further." Carlyle singled out Cabanis for special attack: "He fairly lays open our moral structure with his dissecting knives and real metal probes . . . he finds nothing real but the saltpetre, pasteboard, and catgut. His book may be regarded as the ultimatum of mechanical metaphysics in our time."[3]

Amid this gloomy vision of technology, materialism, and cynicism, Carlyle found hope in the organic and dynamic, the "celestial birthright" of mankind. The history of all far-reaching movements, he pointed out, is a history of invisible, vital, ideal aims. Christianity arose "in the mystic deeps of man's soul"; it was spread abroad by "simple, altogether natural and individual efforts." Even the French Revolution "had something higher in it than cheap bread and a Habeas-Corpus Act. Here too was an Idea; a Dynamic, not a Mechanic Force." True science and art, Carlyle observed, have been created not by institutions and guilds and vested interests but by the inner soul of the individual.

He developed this contrast further in *Sartor Resartus* and in *Heroes and Hero-Worship*. "I, for my share," he wrote, "declare the world to be no machine! I say that it does *not* go by wheel-and-pinion 'motives,' self-interests, checks, balances; that there is something far other in it than the clank of spinning-jennies and parliamentary majorities." For this reason he found the ancient Norse mythology attractive:[4]

[3] Thomas Carlyle, *The Works of Thomas Carlyle* (Charles Scribner's Sons, London, 1897–1901), XXVII, 59–65.
[4] *Ibid.*, V, 20–21.

All life is figured by them as a tree. Igdrasil, the Ash-tree of Existence, has its roots deep-down in the kingdoms of Hela or Death;
its trunk reaches up heaven-ward, spreads its boughs over the
whole Universe. . . . Is not every leaf of it a biography, every
fibre there an act or word? Its boughs are Histories of Nations.
. . . Considering how human things circulate, each inextricably
in communion with all—how the word I speak to you today is
borrowed, not from Ulfinal the Moesogoth only, but from all men
since the first man began to speak—I find no similitude so true as
this of a Tree. Beautiful; altogether beautiful and great. The
"Machine of the Universe"—alas, do but think of that in contrast!

Unlike some of his contemporaries, however, Carlyle recognized that the organic and the mechanical were comple-
mentary aspects of the complexity inherent in civilization.
Real progress would come, he thought, only through attaining
an effective balance between the two. He believed that
cleavage between them would lead to idle visions on the
one hand and to pernicious materialism on the other. The
latter he took to be "the grand characteristic" of his age.[5]

What was probably the predominant American reaction to
Carlyle's essay may be discovered in Timothy Walker's
critique of it in the *North American Review* of July, 1831.[6]
Walker, a prominent lawyer, felt that Carlyle was a misguided mystic. "In plain words," he wrote, "we deny the evil
tendencies of Mechanism, and we doubt the good influences
of his Mysticism." As for the psychology of Locke: "Give us
Locke's Mechanism, and we will envy no man's Mysticism.
Give us to know 'the origin of our ideas,' to comprehend the
phenomena 'which we see in the mind,' and we will leave the
question of the mind's essence to transcendental speculators."

[5] *Ibid.,* XXVII, 73.
[6] *North American Review,* XXXIII (July, 1831), 122–26. Portions of
Walker's critique are reprinted in Miller, *The Transcendentalists,* pp.
40–43.

Finally, Walker saw no danger that man's inner faculties might become standardized and inert in a machine age; on the contrary, he anticipated a new golden age of culture as a result of the industrial revolution. With technological improvements increasing leisure time, there would be nothing to hinder all men from becoming poets and philosophers.

Against Walker's review, the voice of common sense, we may place the pronouncements contained in *The Dial*, the most famous organ of the small but highly articulate group of "transcendental speculators." The introductory announcement in the initial issue of July, 1840, written by Margaret Fuller and rewritten by Emerson, established their position:

And so with diligent hands and good intent we set down our Dial on the earth. . . . Let it be such a Dial, not as the dead face of a clock, hardly even such as the Gnomon in a garden, but rather such a Dial as is the Garden itself, in whose leaves and flowers and fruits the suddenly awakened sleeper is instantly apprised not what part of dead time, but what state of life and growth is now arrived and arriving.

This proclamation reminds us of Lovejoy's definition of Romanticism as "a conviction that the world is an *englischer Garten* on a grand scale,"[7] and it might well serve as one of the central statements of the American Romantic movement. A later issue contained an article entitled "Prophecy—Transcendentalism—Progress," in which Emerson cautioned his contemporaries that the outward manifestations of progress they saw all about them would be meaningless and even dangerous if they were not accompanied by equal inner growth in the souls of individuals. In an argument strongly reminiscent of Carlyle's "Signs of the Times," Emerson defined the conflict between the mechanical and the organic

[7] *The Great Chain of Being*, p. 16.

as the fundamental issue of the age, one that underlay controversies in every field of human concern.[8]

A brief glance at the writings of Emerson's New England contemporaries in some of these fields will confirm his conclusion. In psychology the theories of Locke, the English empiricists, and the French materialists were lumped together and branded as mechanical. "Is man nothing but a combination of five senses, a thinking machine, to grind up and bolster sensations?" cried out Theodore Parker.[9] Against Locke's conception of the mind as a slatelike recorder and reorganizer of sense perceptions, Sampson Reed opposed a psychology that, as the title of his short but influential *Observations on the Growth of the Mind* (first published in 1826) indicates, was based upon the organic metaphor. He considered the mind to be a "delicate germ" that grows not from external accretion or through uniform laws of association but from an internal principle that differs in each individual.[10] The acid test of this psychology—and an early prelude to the present long-winded but important controversy over progressive education—occurred in the school conducted by Bronson Alcott and Elizabeth Peabody. Abandoning the time-honored practice of regarding children as small vacuums to be filled with uniform amounts of information, Alcott sought to educate his flock by drawing out their individual responses to leading questions. The basic premise of his pedagogy was eloquently summed up by Miss Peabody in the conclusion to her *Record of a School* (1835).[11]

There is something at the foundation of the human soul, analogous to the organization of a plant. We may assist a plant, if we will

[8] *The Dial*, II (July, 1841), 83–121.
[9] Miller, *The Transcendentalists*, p. 319.
[10] *Observations on the Growth of the Mind* (Crosby, Nichols and Company, Boston, 1838), pp. 22–31.
[11] Reprinted in Miller, *The Transcendentalists*, pp. 149–50.

study its nature, but there are things which might be put around one plant, which would destroy another. And so we may assist a soul; but there is only one way. We must study its nature. . . . Then we shall find that each soul has a form, a beauty, a purpose of its own. And we shall also find, that there are a few general conditions never to be shut out: that, as the light of heaven, the warmth of earth, and space to expand, are necessary to the plants; so knowledge of God, the sympathy of human love, and liberty to act from within outward, are indispensable to the soul.

In the crucial field of religion, the same metaphor supported the radical revolt against rationalism. Orestes Brownson saw the religious movements of his time as a process of death and rebirth; Unitarianism had accomplished the necessary task of destroying Calvinism, he felt, but it was now time for the "organic" phase to begin. In the Transcendental doctrine (this was written before his conversion to Catholicism in 1844), Brownson found "the germ of re-organization," a nucleus for a new moral and religious world. Theodore Parker carried the attack on historical Christianity even further. In his trenchant "Discourse of the Transient and Permanent in Christianity," he argued that "real Christianity gives men new life. It is the growth and perfect action of the Holy Spirit God puts into the sons of men." The special doctrines of each sect, therefore, were merely transitory and should be sloughed off like dead leaves with changing times. The part of Parker's sermon that most profoundly shocked the congregation at South Boston Church was his emphasis upon the divine element in each individual. "It is not so much by the Christ who lived so blameless and beautiful eighteen centuries ago that we are saved directly," he said, "but by the Christ we form in our hearts and live in our daily life."[12] Such an extreme position could not be tolerated, even though

12 *Ibid.*, p. 279. For an illuminating discussion of the issues that

HAWTHORNE'S TRAGIC VISION

Parker was well liked; and he was ostracized from the Boston churches.

The conflict in science was less heated, though its implications for the future were more significant. That the objects and processes of nature could not be comprehended unless they were studied in their actual, living connections—an idea that became firmly established only after Darwin's achievement in *The Origin of Species* (1859)—was, of course, a constant theme in the writings of both Emerson and Thoreau. "I hate museums," asserted Thoreau. "They are dead nature collected by dead men."[13] His spirit rebelled against artificial classifications, against the unreal isolation of the dissecting room and the laboratory, against the rigid application of formulas to natural phenomena. Although he stressed the necessity for precise observation, he constantly sought a synthesis that would give meaning to his data. More of an artist than a scientist, he came closer to being both than any other Romanticist except Goethe. As Alcott once noted in his journal, Thoreau was "rightly named Thorough, Through, the pervading Thor, the sturdy sensibility and force in things."[14]

It is unnecessary to accumulate further evidence showing that the conflict between the organic and the mechanical became a bifocal lens through which all phenomena could be viewed, or to comment on the ironic fact that in eliminating the older dualism between mind and matter the Romanticists substituted one of their own making. In theory, as Emerson contended, this antithesis, along with all others, could be

---

separated Brownson and Parker, see R. W. B. Lewis, *The American Adam*, pp. 174–89.

[13] *The Writings of Henry David Thoreau* (Houghton Mifflin Company, Boston, 1906), VII, 464.

[14] *The Journals of Bronson Alcott*, ed. Odell Shepard (Little, Brown & Company, Boston, 1938), p. 315.

The Organic-Mechanical Antithesis

resolved in a higher synthesis: the unity of nature encompassed both poles. But as he surveyed the most spectacular triumphs of mechanism in this country, the technological advances, he was plagued with misgivings. He was capable of asserting that "machinery and Transcendentalism agree well. Stagecoach and Railroads are bursting the old legislation, like green withes."[15] But this expansive optimism was extreme even for Emerson, whose more characteristic attitude was summed up in his aphorism, "Things are in the saddle and ride mankind."

More revealing than any abstract statement is the tension the two contraries could generate within such works of art as Melville's stories. The maimed Ahab, who cries out that the path of his fixed purpose is laid with "iron rails" and who sardonically orders the blacksmith to fashion a massive ideal man with a brass forehead, no heart, and copious brains, is unalterably determined to mutilate and dissect the white whale, whose awesome and inscrutable vitality is eternal and ubiquitous. Not only in *Moby Dick* but also in "The Bell Tower" and "The Tartarus of Maids," Melville clearly anticipated D. H. Lawrence's dread of the machine as a numbing, atrophying agent. "The machine is the great neuter," Lawrence wrote, as he strove to escape it in the mountains of New Mexico. "In the end it emasculates us all."[16] Ahab's injury, as Richard Chase has abundantly shown,[17] is a kind of symbolic castration that is contrasted with Ishmael's idealization of the life-giving sperm.

[15] *Journals of Ralph Waldo Emerson*, ed. Edward Waldo Emerson and Waldo Emerson Forbes (Houghton Mifflin Company, Boston, 1909–14), VI, 397.

[16] *Studies in Classic American Literature* (Albert & Charles Boni, Inc., New York, 1930), p. 186.

[17] *Herman Melville: A Critical Study* (The Macmillan Company, New York, 1949), pp. 42–45.

Although the events of "The Bell Tower" take place in Italy during the early Renaissance, its theme makes it a fable for mid-nineteenth-century America. In its cryptic, curiously passive prose, the story demonstrates the negation of life in a society led by a "practical materialist." The tower is a "stone pine," its bells "a metallic aviary," and its architect "the great mechanician" Bannadonna. He secretly creates, as a device for tolling the hours, a robot resembling Ahab's proposed mechanical man. This automaton is merely a partial type of what he hopes eventually to achieve in Talus, the "iron slave" who will perform all of man's work. But what was to have been Bannadonna's greatest triumph turns out to be his destruction; as the crowd eagerly awaits the first tolling of the bell, they hear only a "dull, mangled sound." The mechanician has been crushed by his own invention, and later, at his funeral, the "groined belfry" crashes to the ground. This, Melville indicates, is the outcome when common sense becomes theurgy; "machinery, miracle; Prometheus, the heroic name for machinist; man, the true God."

That a similar idea (with a shift in gender) motivates "The Tartarus of Maids" needs to be established in slightly more detail, since critical comment on this sketch seems to be somewhat misleading. The narrator, who describes himself as a "seedsman," travels toward a paper mill near Woedolor Mountain in New England. As E. H. Eby first observed over fifteen years ago,[18] the approach to the mountain is described in imagery that relates the landscape to the female body. It should also be noted that the whole country, locked in the depth of winter, looks like "one petrifaction." The seedsman's sleigh grits over the snow "as if it had been broken glass." The trees groan in the fitful gusts of the wind, and, "brittle with excessive frost, many colossal, tough-grained maples,

[18] *Modern Language Quarterly*, I (March, 1940), 95–100.

The Organic-Mechanical Antithesis

snapped in twain like pipe-stems, cumbered the unfeeling earth." The mountains are like shrouds—"a pass of Alpine corpses." This description of the white death that has settled over the once-vital countryside prepares us for the "large, whitewashed factory" and for the "various, rude, irregular squares and courts" that comprise the boardinghouses of the workers. Owing to the "broken, rocky nature of the ground," there is no unity of arrangement here.

Once inside the paper mill, the seedsman discovers "rows of blank-looking girls, with blank white folders in their blank hands, all blankly folding blank paper." The papermaking process, as Eby discerned, is a monstrous symbol of gestation. It takes nine minutes for the slip of paper marked "Cupid" to travel from the vats of white pulp, "the first beginnings," to the end, which is "a sort of paper-fall, not wholly unlike a water-fall; a scissory sound smote my ear, as of some cord being snapped; and down dropped an unfolded sheet of perfect foolscap." Judging from these grotesque images, Eby argued that Melville's main intention was "to represent through the medium of the story the biological burdens imposed upon women because they bear the children." But the point is that these "passive-looking girls" do *not* bear children; married women do not work here—"they are apt to be off-and-on too much." The maidens have been sterilized by the "inflexible iron animal" that has usurped their fertility. Thus the papermaking process becomes a ghastly mockery of the maidens' plight; as they are blanked out in an icy living death, the parasitic machine sucks their vital force, labors, and gives birth to foolscap. Even the narrator's cheeks "look whitish" after his brief exposure to the leechlike "panting Behemoth."

It is hard to see how the attack on mechanism could be carried any further. One allusion shows how Melville's story is related to the broader conflict whose outlines we have traced. As the seedsman watches the paper dropping from the machine, he cannot help thinking of John Locke and his comparison of the human mind to a sheet of blank paper, "something destined to be scribbled upon." The implication is unmistakable: Locke's psychology perfectly matches the mechanism of the mill. The notion that sense impressions follow one another and become agglutinated through uniform laws of mental gravitation finds a perfect parallel in the "metallic necessity, the unbudging fatality" that governs the papermaking machinery.

Melville's marginalia in his copy of Emerson's essays illustrate his approval of the organic theory of art.[19] But he knew that the "silent, grass-growing mood" was only half the composing process. The pressing-out of a bold, nervous, and lofty language required painful intellectual effort and emotional involvement—an aspect of composition that demanded a different metaphor, the hell-fire of the try works. And Melville found Emerson's ethical pronouncements hollow because he knew that men's hearts, like their artistic expression, must be purified by the fire of tragic experience. Ishmael starts his voyage on the *Pequod* entertaining the half-serious belief that hell is an idea fostered by dyspepsia. By the time he is rescued at the end, he knows better.

We know from Melville's correspondence, if from no other source, that Hawthorne would have said "Amen" to his younger friend's critique of Emerson and Goethe. And we shall eventually conclude our discussion of Hawthorne's attitude toward the Romantic promise by observing that he too found the "furnace" necessary for artistic and moral conversion. But it would fatally distort the delicate balance of

[19] See F. O. Matthiessen, *American Renaissance* (Oxford University Press, New York, 1941), p. 185.

The Organic-Mechanical Antithesis

Hawthorne's fiction if we overlooked the strong pull the organic metaphor exerted upon him.

Familiar with the writings of Goethe, Coleridge, and Carlyle, conversant with Channing, Emerson, Hillard, and Thoreau, Hawthorne could hardly have missed being exposed to the ideas stemming from the fundamental belief that the universe was a coherent, living unit. He habitually, almost compulsively, referred to himself and his work as organic: the *Twice-Told Tales* he likened to "flowers which blossomed in too retired a shade"; the tales and sketches in *Mosses from an Old Manse* "blossomed out like flowers in the calm summer" of his "heart and mind"; and "the ripened autumnal fruit" was gathered in *The Snow-Image*. These were harvested by an author who often compared himself to the hawthorn bush of a pastoral or to a dubious bough on the family tree.

Such metaphors may seem casual and conventional at first glance. However, they point to the Romantic strain that runs throughout Hawthorne's fiction.[20] He had been schooled in the prose style of Addison and Steele, and as a boy he had admired Boswell's portrait of Dr. Johnson. But as he grew older, he came to consider Johnson a "one-eyed man," and he rebelled as vehemently as Coleridge or Emerson against the mechanical tenets of the early eighteenth century. He detested attempts to reduce religion to theology, psychology to biology, morality and art to mathematical principles. A slight but revealing glimpse of this attitude is furnished in his account of his first visit to Ticonderoga, when he had for a guide a young West Point lieutenant. The guide's description was "as accurate as a geometrical theorem," but it

[20] See Roy R. Male, " 'From the Innermost Germ': The Organic Principle in Hawthorne's Fiction," *Journal of English Literary History,* XX (September, 1953), 218–36.

stripped the old fort of all human and historical significance. "His lectures on ravelins, counterscarps, angles, and covered ways, made it an affair of brick and mortar and hewn stone, arranged on certain regular principles, having a good deal to do with mathematics, but nothing at all with poetry" (III, 592).

Hawthorne's criticism of eighteenth-century thought naturally centered on the problem of artistic creation. "The Artist of the Beautiful," though it was probably not intended as such, can be read as a parable of the Romantic transition. It is not merely that Owen Warland (whose last name, of course, suggests his struggle against the materialism of the "hard, coarse world") is an "irregular genius" set over against Peter Hovenden, whose psychology of the five senses is as much Lockian as it is Yankee. The whole plot consists of a series of oppositions that bulk large in the writings of Coleridge and other Romanticists: the useful and the beautiful, the material and the ideal, the mechanical and the organic, understanding and imagination.[21] The major symbols, in addition to their function in the story, have historical significance as well. Warland's apprenticeship and his periods of artistic sterility are spent in the clock world, characteristic symbol of that period when, as Coleridge put it, the "discoveries of Newton ... gave almost a religious sanction to the corpuscular and mechanical theory." The butterfly, on the other hand, aptly represents the Romantic ideal of beauty: its ancient association with the psyche is in full accord with the subjectivity inherent in Romantic aesthetic theory; furthermore, it spectacularly demonstrates the metamorphosis

[21] See Richard Harter Fogle, *Hawthorne's Fiction: The Light and the Dark* (University of Oklahoma Press, Norman, Okla., 1952), pp. 70–78. Hereafter cited as *Hawthorne's Fiction*.

Emerson called "the law of the universe." Owen's artistic creation begins as a lifeless mechanism but transcends this state to attain a life of its own, "a spiritual essence—call it magnetism or what you will" (II, 534).

Hawthorne's story illustrates the fact that the essential issue separating neoclassic and Romantic literature was also the ever present condition of the artist's life in America. His portrait of the artist is, it must be admitted, a miniature; Warland is too frail and lacks the intellectual discipline and tough pertinacity that saved Hawthorne himself from self-pity and frustration. Warland personifies what Emerson called the "double consciousness," the worst feature of which was that "the two lives, of the understanding and of the soul . . . really show very little relation to each other." Hawthorne was to return to this cleavage in American culture in *The Blithedale Romance,* where the gap between art and experience proved to be one reason for the failure of the Blithedale experiment.

Hawthorne contrasted the delicate fragility of Warland's art with the solid strength of the blacksmith's work. His own art, at its best, combined the two. Like Melville, he felt that the organic metaphor beautifully expressed both the initial "germ" and the final product of composition. But it failed to convey the torment and the sense of accomplishment that came from rendering raw material and heated thoughts into malleable form. In this mood the artist is more like Ethan Brand, projecting his dark ideas into the glowing furnace. Fire, like sin and suffering, is both destructive and creative; it is an "angel or fiend, double in his nature, and capable of deeds befitting both characters" (II, 451). It was precisely this element, this image of the fiery crucible, which Hawthorne and Melville found lacking in Emerson's theories of art and morality. The difference between Emerson and Hawthorne, which amounted to almost total lack of communication, may be summed up in their descriptions of those intuitive moments when truth is perceived.

Emerson's intuitions came outside his home—as he crossed a bare common or walked in the woods. Here a man could cast off time as a snake sloughs his skin; here he could find freedom in space and perpetual youth. "In the woods," he wrote in the famous passage in *Nature,* "we return to reason and faith. There I feel that nothing can befall me in life—no disgrace, no calamity (leaving me my eyes,) which nature cannot repair. Standing on the bare ground,—my head bathed by the blithe air, and uplifted into infinite space,—all mean egotism vanishes. I become a transparent eyeball." We know from Hawthorne's "Buds and Bird Voices" and "The New Adam and Eve" how deeply he wished this paean to spring and eternal youth could be true. But he would finally conclude that Emerson's angle of vision was one-eyed. It is the perspective of boyhood and is appropriate to youth. But for maturity, something must "befall"; the very "disgraces and calamities" for which Emerson sought Nature's therapy are the heart of moral life.

Hawthorne's own characteristic stance was that of a man peering into the domestic fireplace, observing its lights and shadows and the gradual conversion of wood into embers and coals. "At such an hour, and with this scene before him, if a man sitting all alone, cannot dream strange things, and make them look like truth, he need never try to write romances" (V, 56). He agreed with the Transcendentalists that moral reform must come from within. But their efforts at transformation without tragedy he branded with their own favorite term of opprobrium: "mechanical." For, as he pointed out in "The Celestial Railroad," so long as man tries to obliterate the Slough of Despond, his schemes of reform

The Organic-Mechanical Antithesis

are merely superficial paving. Fire may destroy; but without it, purification of "that inward sphere" is impossible. Until this truth is fully comprehended, the Romantic categories "organic" and "mechanical" remain ambiguous terms in art and ethics.

iii ⁓

The Search for a Home

STEEPED IN THE HISTORY of his province and armed with a penetrating insight that was sharpened by the critical principles of his time, Hawthorne wrote the myth of New England. If his stories were arranged according to the date of their action, they would cover more than two centuries, from the settlement at Merry Mount to the formation of Brook Farm. His own awareness of this aspect of his fiction, his role as critic and interpreter of the past, may be seen in "Main Street" (1849), a kind of romancer's allegory in which he assumed the guise of a showman to describe his efforts at imaginatively reconstructing the history of New England. "I have contrived a certain pictorial exhibition, somewhat in the nature of a puppet-show," he wrote, with the wry humor characteristic of his self-criticism," by means of which I propose to call up the multiform and many-colored Past before the spectator." Ironically suggesting that his hard-won stories had been turned out "with no greater trouble than the turning of a crank," Hawthorne subjected his vision of the past, with its manipulation of light and shadow, imagery and atmosphere, to the criticism of two onlookers. One is a literal historian who mildly objects to the numerous anachronisms; the other is an "acidulous-looking gentleman" who insists upon "seeing things as they are" through his blue glasses and refuses to take the "proper point of view."

From the stories of early New England and from such sketches as "Main Street," Hawthorne's legend can be briefly summarized. It begins with the primitive forest, ruled over by the great squaw Sachem and her magician husband, Wappacowet. With the advent of the first English settlers comes a presentiment that the wild, dynamic harmony of savage and nature will be stamped out. "The pavements of the Main Street must be laid over the red man's grave." The first generation of Puritans were men like Endicott, resolute of purpose, stern of mien. In the conflict between the two settlements of Plymouth and Merry Mount could be seen the cost of destroying the savage culture and of leaving behind the traditions that had enriched life in Old England. "Jollity and gloom contended for an empire": on the one hand were the silken colonists of Merry Mount, whose "systematic gayety" consisted of a sophisticated imitation of primitive fertility rites; on the other were the Puritan men of iron, whose inhibition of sex and gloomy view of life centered around the barren counterpart of the Maypole, the whipping post.

The sword of Hawthorne's Endicott leveled the living pine

tree that had been festooned as a Maypole; it also ripped the red cross from the flag of England in an assertion of religious freedom. Both were necessary steps; but, as mirrored in the shining breastplate of the Puritan, this "freedom" seemed more like a distorted bigotry to such dissidents as Roger Williams and Anne Hutchinson. With the passing of the first generation, religious gloom was maintained with only a counterfeit of the earlier religious ardor. Life in the somber years that followed became "sinister to the intellect and sinister to the heart." The solid piety of the early Puritans was transmuted into neurotic persecutions of Quakers and witches; the home of Sachem and Wappacowet became the realm of the Black Man, whose devious workings in the souls of men were dramatized as a logical procession in the jeremiads from the pulpit.

It is clear that Hawthorne knew the history of New England well enough to imagine it symbolically without doing any essential injustice to the facts. He gave shape to the bare chronicles of names and events by envisaging the dialectic between theocracy and wilderness as a "spontaneous allegory" representing the rhythm of human life. The wilderness offered freedom from time's ravages, a dream of renascent youth, but it was also the realm of the devil. Since in its untrammeled spaciousness no guiding path from past experience could be discerned, what appeared to be freedom was likely to prove delusory wandering and waste. The theocracy was also ambiguous. It preserved some of the values from the past, but in the rigorous effort of splintering off from England and leveling the forest, the Puritans had steeled themselves against any further novelty or diversity. If the wilderness promised a dream of youth that might become a nightmare, the theocracy assumed the views of premature old age.

With the gradual disintegration of the theocracy and the

triumph of the youthful spirit began the quest for a home that has stirred Americans ever since. If a study of the house as symbol in American literature were undertaken, certainly one conclusion would be that the home has consistently represented, whether consciously or not, an attempt to build an integrated, functioning religious experience: a fusion of time and space, investment and speculation, past and present. The only discernible tie, for example, among such disparate figures as Whitman, Poe, and Emily Dickinson is their common effort to build their own religion. Whitman found himself in his role as second Adam: tearing down the door jambs, watching the corpse of the past as it was carried out of the house, constantly changing his perspective as he moved down the open road. But in his best poetry he balanced this disintegrating impulse by finally accepting time on his own terms, discovering it in the cradle of his childhood experience and in a firmer knowledge of death. Poe's role is established by the epithet most often applied to him: "that poor devil." A figure in a black cape presiding over the disintegration of the psyche, abolishing all ethical meaning from art and criticism as didactic heresy, Poe and his diabolism are typified by the inverted image of the house of Usher, reflected eerily in the tarn. Emily Dickinson's characteristic vestment, on the other hand, was white, and she built herself a role as empress of Calvary, bride of Christ. "Some keep the Sabbath going to Church—/I keep it staying at home," she wrote. Her most memorable poem, beginning "Because I could not stop for Death," centers around the journey to the final house of time, the grave.

In such a study Hawthorne's fiction would occupy a large place. In his own life he restlessly sought a home that would combine the rich density of accumulated time with freedom and novelty of open space. From Salem, rich but oppressive in ancestral tradition, he escaped to the Maine woods, to Bowdoin, Boston, Brook Farm, and Concord. In his later years he felt an irresistible pull back toward the center: to his birthplace, to "our old home" in England, and to Rome, "the city of all time." But he was always fearful that life would become "fossilized" (VII, 78). Once nourished by his communion with catholic antiquity, he was eager to return to "The Wayside."

The interaction of past and present, stasis and movement always fascinated him. Ceremonies, rituals, and processions almost invariably invoked some of his most unforgettable scenes: the fertility rites of the colonists at Merry Mount that made their "true history a poet's tale," the Election Day procession in *The Scarlet Letter,* the masquerade at Blithedale, and the carnival in *The Marble Faun.* These ceremonies were appealing partly because they expressed mankind's yearning for "real principles of union," for a remnant of the ancient tribal communal. Even the political procession in *The House of the Seven Gables* shares some of this quality. Viewed from a distance it seems a majestic symbol of a common inheritance. "It melts all the petty personalities, of which it is made up, into one broad mass of existence—one great life,—one collected body of mankind, with a vast homogeneous spirit animating it." The appeal of this spirit for Clifford Pyncheon is almost irresistible. On the other hand, the crowd may display a callous cruelty, as in the climactic scene of "My Kinsman, Major Molineux," where the people behave "like fiends that throng in mockery around some dead potentate, mighty no more but majestic still in his agony" (III, 640).

In the rituals and ceremonies of his time Hawthorne saw typified the ambiguous benefits of a progressive civilization in which "words have been feebly substituted in the place of

The Search for a Home

signs and symbols" (VI, 97). These affairs preserved some
vestige of the past; but their artificiality seemed almost to
mock man's efforts to recover the primal vitality that had
virtually dried up in commonplace prosperity, intellectual
analysis, and mechanical morality. Observing the empty ceremonies in Salem on November 5, he remarked that the young
men lit bonfires "in commemoration of they know not what."
Cut off from tradition, Americans are "a people of the present, and have no heartfelt interest in the olden times" (XII,
280).

Nothing is more painful than forced merriment or feigned
religious fervor, and Hawthorne was quick to perceive evi-
dences of both not only in this country but also abroad. While
he deeply admired the beauty and the religious symbolism of
the English Gothic cathedrals, he was repelled by the Episco-
pal services, considering them a corruption of Roman Catholicism. "After all," he wrote, "the rites are lifeless in our day"
(*English Notebooks*, 257).[1] His patience was sorely tried by
the Easter services at York Cathedral; numb with cold, he sat
through the seemingly endless ceremony, reflecting that the
ornate beauty seemed to join with the elaborate music and
the rich ceremonial in detracting from the effectiveness of
the sermon. These were "externals, into which religious life
had first gushed and flowered, and then petrified" (*English
Notebooks*, 451). Never had his sympathies been more in
accord with his Puritan ancestors.

Hawthorne's attitude toward Roman Catholicism was am-
bivalent. Acknowledging the psychological effectiveness of
the confessional, he also appreciated the tenderness of a
religion centered upon the Virgin Mother. "There are many

---

[1] *The English Notebooks by Nathaniel Hawthorne*, ed. Randall
Stewart (Modern Language Association of America, New York, 1941).
Hereafter cited as *English Notebooks*.

things in the religious customs of these people that seem good," he wrote in *The Marble Faun,* "many things, at least, that might be both good and beautiful, if the soul of goodness and the sense of beauty were as much alive in the Italians now as they must have been when those customs were first imagined and adopted" (VI, 343). But he was repelled by the intrusive masculinity, which he felt to be out of place in a religion whose function of conserving the values of the past should have been essentially feminine. The very ingenuity of Catholicism made him suspicious of its "pious strategy." With its remedy for every conceivable human weakness, with its Jesuit priests who know "how to work each proper engine," what a religion it would be "if there were but angels to work it, instead of the very different class of engineers who now manage its cranks and safety-valves" (VI, 393). When the thought occurs to Kenyon that the shrines of the Virgin might well be adorned by flower pots with living plants, he finally rejects the idea. "Their worship nowadays," he said of the Italians, "is best symbolized by the artificial flower" (VI, 343). Similarly, he felt that the carnival, which "was the pastime and the earnest of a more innocent and homelier age," had now become commercialized and existed chiefly for the benefit of English and American tourists.

The "venal and polluted flowers" of the Roman carnival, sold by the basketful on the Corso, symbolized the problem that had long plagued Hawthorne as he watched his own country in transition from wilderness to civilization. With each successive generation after the settlements were laid over the red man's grave, the mystery and wildness of spirit he recognized as an essential part of humanity seemed in danger of drying up. Though the earliest Puritans were narrow and rigid, they at least were in earnest. There was "nothing forced or feigned" about their fast days or their

The Search for a Home

Election Week; the crowd that gathered to witness Hester Prynne's disgrace was severe but "had none of the heartlessness of another social state, which would find only a theme for jest" in such an exhibition.

Hawthorne's search for a home, then, was his effort to combine the masculine protestant vision of America with the feminine catholic communion of Europe in a religious faith broad enough for the Pantheon (which provides the setting at the end of *The Marble Faun*). Actually, of course, he attempted no such simultaneous combination as an intellectual system or theology; rather, he knew that these opposites were a narrative rhythm, a temporal cycle beginning with rebellion against the ancestral burden and ending with acceptance of it, with various "epiphanies" along the way. A theme that occupied him in some of his earliest work and again in his last fragmentary romances—the search for a home—may be illustrated by two stories, "The Gentle Boy," and "My Kinsman, Major Molineux." Both have historical settings that merge unobtrusively with the problem of moral and psychological growth.

It is easy to underestimate Hawthorne's solid achievement in "The Gentle Boy." Although the story has been popular ever since its first publication in *The Token* in 1832, too often it is read simply as a tract against Puritan bigotry and Quaker fanaticism in the seventeenth century. A more careful reading will show, I think, that the story's subject is the agonizing difficulty of finding an integrated, fruitful religious experience in America—the difficulty, that is to say, of finding a home. Hawthorne carefully delineates the religious structure of the society into which Ilbrahim, the Gentle Boy, will be introduced. Two groups emphasize the supernatural, but their values are sharply opposed. The Puritans are chiefly concerned with manifestations of the devil, and their view of life is typified by the minister's black skullcap. Systematic and dignified, they find a home in the meetinghouse, where the sexes are split apart. The Quakers, on the other hand, are enthusiastic, imaginative, and irrational. Their equally incomplete view of life is symbolized in the "deathly whiteness" of Catherine, the fanatic. Their home is the wilderness. Between the Puritans, "who have shunned the cross" and the Quakers, who are obsessed by their own martyrdom, is Tobias Pearson, who wears "gray frieze" and is more concerned with this world than the next. He has come to this country for economic rather than religious reasons, and it is to "this supposed impurity of motive" that the Puritans attribute the death of his children. But he does feel an inadequacy in his religion, a need for a more "fervid faith." He is never really converted to either the Puritan or the Quaker cause.

As Catherine observes toward the end of the story, life under these conditions is a gradual crucifixion. Probably the most agonizing experience for a parent is the loss of a child; certainly the most painful experience for a child is the loss of a parent. And the broken home is the dominant pattern in the story. Dorothy and Tobias lose their children, Ilbrahim loses his father, Catherine loses her child, the old Quaker has left his daughter on her deathbed, and the Puritan meetinghouse splits the parents.

Into this splintered existence comes a saving remnant, the Gentle Boy. In describing Ilbrahim, whose "outlandish" Turkish name indicates his divinely redemptive qualities, Hawthorne looks back to Isaiah and forward to Melville. As Tobias Pearson proceeds homeward, he hears the voice of one crying in the wilderness. "The voice is most likely mortal," he says to himself, "nor have I cause to tremble if it is otherwise." Finding a child beneath the gallows tree, which resembles a cross, he asks for his name and his home. "They call me Ilbrahim, and my home is here," says the child, pointing to his father's grave. In this haunting reply, a passage marked by Melville, lies the probable genesis of "Call me Ishmael." Ilbrahim, the innocent scapegoat who becomes the savior, is an anticipation of Billy Budd. Only "the process of time" and the tragic sacrifice of an innocent too pure for this world will soften the once-bitter Puritan persecutors and teach the wandering parent a "true religion."

Though the story ends on a note of tough hopefulness, Hawthorne's emphasis rests upon the suffering rather than the bliss of purification. Caught between two narrow faiths, Tobias Pearson acts according to the simplest Christian ethic and is crushed by the consequences of his action.[2] In this story, as in Hawthorne's other fiction, there is no simple formula for moral growth.

Thus, of all the echoes from Isaiah and Jeremiah that reverberate throughout "The Gentle Boy," perhaps the key-note is set by Jeremiah's cry: "Oh that I had in the wilderness a lodging-place of wayfaring men" (IX, 2). In this lacerated society, the word "home" becomes a talisman. When he first published the story in *The Token,* Hawthorne introduced Pearson's journey by writing that "a gloomy extent of nearly four miles lay between him and his *house.*" In revising the story for *Twice-Told Tales* (1837), he changed "house" to "home." As Seymour L. Gross has observed in his study of Hawthorne's revisions, this seemingly unimportant change points up a series of other references to "home."[3] Perhaps it accounts for Hawthorne's deletion of a richly detailed

[2] See Louise Dauner, "The 'Case' of Tobias Pearson: Hawthorne and the Ambiguities," *American Literature,* XXI (January, 1950), 468–69.

[3] "Hawthorne's Revision of 'The Gentle Boy,'" *American Literature,* XXVI (May, 1954), 196–208.

description of the interior of Pearson's cottage. He omitted this passage, I suspect, because it tended to blur the point that Pearson's home was spiritually empty until Ilbrahim came and empty again after he died.

If Ilbrahim's search is for a mother, Robin's quest, in "My Kinsman, Major Molineux," is for a father. Lionel Trilling has described as the backbone of nineteenth-century fiction such novels as Stendhal's *The Red and the Black,* Balzac's *Père Goriot,* and Dickens' *Great Expectations.*[4] These stories, strongly linked with folk legend, are defined by their heroes, all of whom are variants of the Young Man from the Provinces. Though Hawthorne never wrote such a novel, one of his best short tales is a classic miniature in this genre. All the essential characteristics are contained in "My Kinsman, Major Molineux": the young man of provincial birth and rearing, his trip to the city, his perplexity about the right thing to do, and his search for a "father" amid the dark background of political intrigue.

Robin, a "country-bred" youth of some native intelligence, is the younger son of a rural clergyman. Having been promised a good start in city life by his rich and childless uncle, Major Molineux, he decides at the age of eighteen that it is "high time to begin the world." Clothed in a three-cornered hat and durable rustic garments, carrying a heavy cudgel formed of an "oak sapling, and retaining part of the hardened root," he sets out on a night journey. After crossing the ferry, he enters a New England town that to his eager naïveté seems as confusing and awesome as "London city."

[4] *The Liberal Imagination* (The Viking Press, Inc., New York, 1950), pp. 61–62.

The Search for a Home

What follows is "an evening of ambiguity and weariness," as Robin searches vainly for his wealthy kinsman. He becomes "entangled in a succession of crooked and narrow streets"; he is plunged into the tricky social structure of the town. Clues to the meaning of this nightmarish evening are supplied by the Freudian theory of dream interpretation, which asserts that visions of the father figure may commonly split into two or more images. The first person accosted by Robin is a dignified elderly gentleman with a polished cane who "at regular intervals uttered two successive hems, of a peculiarly sepulchral intonation." To the youth's request for information about Major Molineux, the citizen wrathfully answers: "Let go my garment, fellow! I tell you, I know not the man you speak of. What! I have authority, I have—hem, hem—authority." Since we are later informed that in the past Robin had listened wearily to his father's homilies, it seems probable that this elderly gentleman grotesquely personifies the youth's rebellion against pietistic parental authority. Part of the story's richness results from the ironic disparity between the reaction of the "shrewd youth" and the actual state of affairs. Yet on the psychological level his naïve judgments contain gleams of truth. For if the story is read as a quest for a father, Robin is partly right when he guesses that the sepulchral gentleman is "some country representative," unacquainted with the niceties of town life. Another bizarre image of his father's authority appears in the dull watchman, who tells Robin in no uncertain terms to go "home, vagabond, home!"

These are shapes of what Robin is attempting to leave behind; there are also various forms of the cultured kinsman he is seeking. Scrutinizing each elderly gentleman "in search of the Major's lineaments," the young man encounters many gay and gallant figures. "Embroidered garments of showy colors," youths imitating European gentlemen of the period, and the gorgeous display of goods in the shop windows dazzle him. He receives a "professional welcome" from two of the town's inhabitants. The first, an innkeeper who is "in the second generation from a French Protestant," offers a courteous but shrill invitation to have supper. "The man sees a family likeness! The rogue has guessed that I am related to the Major!" observes Robin, again blind to the actual situation but intuitively right about the unconscious relationship. Needless to say, the innkeeper's attitude changes abruptly when he learns that Robin's wallet contains only threepence and that the youth is seeking Major Molineux, the English governor who is to be driven out of town that very night. A second professional purveyor of hospitality also points up Robin's search for a worldly father. This is the lady of the scarlet petticoat, the Major's "housekeeper," who says, "I bid you hearty welcome in his name." Slyly surveying the youth as he stands in the doorway, she notes his affinity with the Major. "You are the good old gentleman's very picture, and I could swear that was his rainy-weather hat. Also he has garments very much resembling those leather small-clothes." Her dainty beauty and seductive glances tempt Robin within, but just at this precarious moment the stodgy watchman approaches, and the scarlet woman disappears into the house.

Thus as he verges upon maturity the young man's yearnings for freedom from authority and for a worldly patrimony take on exaggerated proportions. The dual aspect of this psychic conflict can be seen in the "infernal visage" of the "double-faced fellow," whose complexions are split. One side of his face is fiery red, emblematic of the military (and of the petticoat); the other is black, representing sepulchral mourn-

The Search for a Home

ing. The grotesque fusion of the two forms is a distorted father image in which youthful misrepresentation of both the real father and the real uncle are combined.

As the evening wears on, the bewildering shades of the false father are gradually counterbalanced by more reliable visions. Robin imagines how this evening has been spent in his own household:

He pictured them assembled at the door, beneath the tree, the great old tree, which had been spared for its huge twisted trunk and venerable shade, when a thousand leafy brethren fell. There, at the going down of the summer sun, it was his father's custom to perform domestic worship, that the neighbors might come and join with him like brothers of the family, and that the wayfaring man might pause to drink at that fountain, and keep his heart pure by freshening the memory of home. Robin distinguished the seat of every individual of the little audience; he saw the good man in the midst, holding the Scriptures in the golden light that fell from the western clouds; he beheld him close the book and all rise up to pray. He heard the old thanksgivings for daily mercies, the old supplications for their continuance, to which he had so often listened in weariness, but which were now among his dear remembrances.

This is the real father, the man who gave his son half the remnant of last year's salary so that the youth could seek his fortune in the city. After this poignant glimpse of what he left behind, the youth is again beset by ambiguities: His mind keeps vibrating between fancy and reality; by turns, the pillars of the balcony lengthen into the tall, bare stems of pines, dwindle down to human figures, settle again to their true shape and size, and then commence a new succession of changes. But Robin is soon awakened from this reverie by another image of the true father, "a gentleman in his prime,

HAWTHORNE'S TRAGIC VISION

of open, intelligent, cheerful, and altogether prepossessing countenance," who becomes a kindly guide. He offers a clue to the bewildering shapes of the town when he suggests that a man may "have several voices, Robin, as well as two complexions," and he stays by the young man's side as the events of the long night reach their awesome climax in the revelation of the wealthy kinsman's actual plight.

Victim of a tar-and-feather procession, the majestic but shaken Major Molineux meets Robin's gaze. "They stared at each other in silence, and Robin's knees shook, and his hair bristled with a mixture of pity and horror." All those who had previously made sport of the youth join in the monstrous procession, weirdly reminiscent of the primitive rites proclaiming the violent overthrow of an old priest-king. Their heartless merriment is contagious, infecting even Robin. Disillusioned in his quest for a worldly inheritance, he laughs louder than anyone else. The mob moves on, "in senseless uproar, in frenzied merriment, trampling all on an old man's heart." Awakened at last, the youth is ready to retreat homeward after this unnerving sight. But, as his friendly counselor suggests, Robin is now mature enough to rise in the world without leaning on an illusory wealthy kinsman.

By placing this story in its historical setting, Hawthorne deftly extends Robin's coming of age so that it applies to the awakening of our national consciousness.[5] With his religious background, his three-cornered hat and blue stockings, Robin becomes a symbol of young Colonial America beginning to break free from its provincial Puritanism and its dependence upon the wealth of England. But the essential elements of the tale emanate from Hawthorne's keen awareness of the

[5] Q. D. Leavis discussed this aspect of the story in "Hawthorne as Poet," *Sewanee Review*, LIX (Spring, 1951), 179–205.

The Search for a Home

"haunted mind." Creating, like the moonlight, "a beautiful strangeness in familiar objects," his imagination took materials from dream fantasy and shaped them into a carefully wrought artistic pattern. Each detail—the great oak tree, Robin's cudgel, the polished cane, the spiked staff, the houses with their many "complexions"—has significance in the story's delicately evoked atmosphere.

✓ imagination

iv ~

The Ambiguity of Beatrice

Hawthorne's ability to create vital women in his fiction is inseparable from his understanding of tragedy. He knew that in order to find a home and a hope of heaven—in order, that is, to develop his full human potential—man must accept either the woman or the dual promise she represents: tragic involvement with sin but also the consequent possibility of redemption. This involvement must be passionate, like Adam's; it is not a matter of rationally selecting the best that can be found in past and present and balancing these elements in an intellectual synthesis. Moral growth occurs in a series of communions in which the bread and wine of the past vitalizes the present.

The Ambiguity of Beatrice

Man is galvanized into moral activity by shocks of recognition in which he sees himself, again as Milton's Adam did, in the tapestry of all time. In "Rappaccini's Daughter" appears the first of Hawthorne's fully developed women—dark, exotic, ambiguous in her "poisonous" combination of sexual attractiveness and angelic purity. Like Hester Prynne, Zenobia, and Miriam in later books, Beatrice Rappaccini is a prototype of womanhood. And the story in which she appears deserves detailed consideration, for it illuminates the best of Hawthorne's other stories and anticipates *The Scarlet Letter*.

The story is almost too complex, too rich in meaning for completely satisfactory analysis. Recurrent images, literary allusions, evocation of tone and atmosphere, structure—every detail in the story is relevant, and to anyone who reads it in this fashion, the conventional interpretation of "Rappaccini's Daughter" as simply illustrating the dangers of intellectual pride is inadequate.[1] As the semiplayful introduction indicates, this is a romance, and a romance by Hawthorne's definition aims at presenting the truth of the human heart. As such, the best gloss for the story can be found elsewhere in *Mosses from an Old Manse*. In "The Intelligence Office" Hawthorne suggests that a study of man's desires—a "Book of Wishes"—would probably be "truer, as a representation of the human heart, than is the living drama of action as it evolves around us. There is more of good and evil in it; more redeeming points of the bad and more errors of the virtuous; higher upsoarings, and baser degradations of the soul; in short, a more perplexing amalgamation of vice and virtue than we witness in the outward world" (II, 377).

"Rappaccini's Daughter" presents just such a "perplexing

[1] For perceptive comments on "Rappaccini's Daughter," see Hyatt Howe Waggoner, *Hawthorne: A Critical Study* (Harvard University Press, Cambridge, Mass., 1955, hereafter cited as *Hawthorne*), pp. 101–17; Fogle, *Hawthorne's Fiction*, pp. 91–103.

amalgamation of vice and virtue." This complexity manifests itself first of all in the objects of the garden, the "Eden of the present world." The plants (not just to Giovanni but to any "wanderer") possess a "questionable and ominous character"; they are unnatural, artificial hybrids resulting from a "commixture and, as it were, adultery, of various vegetable species." They are, in short, human productions like those listed in "The New Adam and Eve," but worse because they mimic God's creations in an "evil mockery of beauty." Their symbolic function is clear: they creep "serpentlike" along the ground; some of them "shock and offend" Beatrice; and Rappaccini avoids their apparently poisonous odors, treating them as though they were deadly snakes.

The same observations would seem to hold for the plant Rappaccini considers the most dangerous of all, the magnificent purple shrub with gemlike blossoms. Yet it is "one shrub in particular" and differs from the other vegetation in several important respects. It is nourished by water from the shattered marble fountain; its brilliance seems "enough to illuminate the garden, even had there been no sunshine"; and it is treated with the utmost affection by Beatrice. The complex symbolic functions of the purple shrub are clarified somewhat by its relation to the water that gushes from the "ruin" of the marble fountain. The water unquestionably symbolizes the spirit, immortal and unaffected by the vicissitudes that have shattered its temporal, earthy vessel. As a unit, the fountain combines the material and the spiritual, but the two are easily distinguishable. Not so with the shrub. It is an ambiguous mixture of matter and spirit, magnificent but poisonous. Fed and reflected by the fountain of the spirit, it nevertheless seems chiefly sensuous in its gorgeous beauty and perfume.

The resplendent shrub, together with its reflection, bathes

The Ambiguity of Beatrice

the garden in a "purple atmosphere" like that of the "Hall of Fantasy," confirming our impression that Rappaccini's garden is a "mystic region, which lies above, below, or beyond the actual" (II, 197). But more important is the way in which it "illuminates" the action that takes place in the garden. For the shrub, like the Great Carbuncle, is different things to different men; like the doubloon in *Moby Dick,* it mirrors men's souls. To Rappaccini, it is an offspring of his intellect, his science. Conceivably it could be regarded as Owen Warland regards his imaginative creation. But Rappaccini, like modern man, fears his scientific production and needs "armor" against it. Beatrice, on the other hand, craves the warmth of love, and to her the ambiguous plant offers the very "breath of life," a token of sisterly affection. Giovanni, though he vacillates, considers the shrub a thing of sensual, if poisonous, beauty, its blossoms to be casually plucked at his pleasure.

The purple shrub is thus a central guide-marker to the action just as it is centrally located in the garden. And it suggests what an analysis of the characters and the action will confirm—that the real subject of the story is the dual nature of humanity: little lower than the angels, yet close to the brutes; potentially almost divine, yet stained with mortal corruption. The fountain symbolizes Beatrice's potential spiritual perfection, the shattered base her mortal clay. And the purple shrub, a brilliant or lurid intermixture of the two, mirrors her paradoxical state since the Fall.

The four protagonists of the story embody in various ways this dualism of good and evil. Rappaccini, as many critics have pointed out, is guilty of intellectual pride and as a result is insecure and out of harmony with nature. Though we have good reason to suspect the motives of his rival, Baglioni, we cannot question his verdict that Rappaccini "cares infinitely

HAWTHORNE'S TRAGIC VISION

more for science than for mankind." But he is by no means a complete villain. As even Baglioni is forced to admit, Rappaccini has occasionally effected a marvelous cure. And his most ambitious, though misguided, experiment—the one involving Giovanni—stems from his laudable desire to bring his daughter's loneliness to an end. Though his physical frame, like that of the marble fountain, is "shattered," he has a "spiritual love" of science.

Baglioni apparently has all the virtues Rappaccini lacks. A jovial man of the world, well aware of the values of good wine, he genially welcomes Giovanni as the son of an old friend. He quite rightly warns the young man of the dangers lurking in Rappaccini's garden; he is not deceived by the seemingly false beauty of Beatrice, and he provides an effective antidote against her poisonous nature. That he is a little jealous of his eminent rival is understandable and human. With Newton Arvin, we may accept him as the representative of "the normal conscience."[2]

But a closer reading reveals something satanic as well. He chuckles and smiles a little too much. The fact that he knew Giovanni's father is not altogether reassuring when we remember the devil's friendship with the father of Young Goodman Brown.[3] And our faint suspicions grow as we realize that Baglioni worships idols just as false as those of Rappaccini. The art of medicine he considers "divine"; his faith rests entirely in its "arcana." He seems to Giovanni to be committing "blasphemy" when he alludes to the "pure and lovely" daughter of Rappaccini. At first admitting that he

[2] *Hawthorne* (Little, Brown & Company, Boston, 1929), p. 138.
[3] This comparison is not so farfetched as it may at first appear. Though "Young Goodman Brown" was written earlier, the two stories were published together in *Mosses from an Old Manse,* and both deal with the same problem: the difficulty of retaining one's faith in a world notable for its ambiguous mixture of good and evil.

blasphemy - the act of expressing the reverence for God

knows little about Beatrice, he later claims to know more than Giovanni and perpetuates the false rumor that she is "learned" in the lore of her father. After the meeting with Rappaccini on the street, Baglioni departs from Giovanni musing to himself in a manner not unlike that of the villain in melodrama: "It is too insufferable an impertinence in Rappaccini, *thus to snatch the lad out of my own hands,* as I may say, and make use of him for his infernal experiments. This daughter of his! It shall be looked to. Perchance, most learned Rappaccini, I may foil you where you little dream of it!" And at the end of the story his tone of triumph reminds one of Aminadab's chuckle at the failure of Aylmer's experiment. If Rappaccini is a hardened, power-mad Aylmer, Baglioni is a subtler, more vicious Aminadab.

There are, therefore, two villains in the story, two polar opposites of evil dominant over good: Rappaccini, inwardly diseased, cut off by intellectual pride from his fellow-man, impious in his attempt to ape God by creating life; and Baglioni, worldly sophisticate, blasphemous in his materialistic skepticism, striving to bring everything "within the limits of ordinary nature"—which for him means the world of the senses. They are static figures, designed to provide a framework for the two central and developing characters of Beatrice and Giovanni.

From the outset Beatrice is, as Waggoner has suggested, the very embodiment of the central Christian paradox—angelic but corrupt, beautiful but damned. The poison in her system, the token of her corruption, brings death into the garden. Unlike Georgiana's relatively innocuous flaw, the poison in Beatrice is ever present and active, bringing death to the beautiful as well as to the ugly. The governess in James's *The Turn of the Screw* describes the two children who are gradually infected with evil as "blameless and foredoomed," and the same terms apply to Beatrice. As the story progresses, however, more and more emphasis is placed on her angelic qualities until at the end she is transformed through death into pure spirit. "Sometimes," wrote Hawthorne in "The Intelligence Office," . . . the spiritual fountain is kept pure by a wisdom within itself and sparkles into the light of heaven without a stain from the earthly strata through which it had gushed upward" (II, 367). This is what happens to Beatrice.

But such a description of her is inadequate, for her deepest significance emerges only in relation to Giovanni's role in the action. He is an ordinary young man in a highly critical situation. For him, Rappaccini's garden becomes an inferno with visions of heaven; it is a decisive test for the wayfaring pilgrim; it is a Bower of Bliss and a Garden of Eden. In short, we see Giovanni undergoing the crucial experience of his Christian life, an experience enriched for us by literary associations drawn from the broad Christian heritage of Dante, Bunyan, Spenser, and Milton. At the very beginning of the story we learn that he has taken lodgings in a chamber of an old Paduan palace, which "exhibited over its entrance the armorial bearings of a family long since extinct. The young stranger, who was not unstudied in the great poem of his country, recollected that one of the ancestors of this family, and perhaps an occupant of this very mansion, had been pictured by Dante as a partaker of the immortal agonies of his Inferno." Hawthorne, like Giovanni, was "not unstudied" in the great poem of Italy,[4] and the allusion to "reminiscences and associations" from *The Divine Comedy,* coming as it does in the first paragraph, is highly suggestive.

[4] For evidence of Hawthorne's familiarity with Dante, see J. C. Matthews, "Hawthorne's Knowledge of Dante," *University of Texas Studies in English,* XX (1940), 157–65.

The Ambiguity of Beatrice

We need not expect rigid correspondences with Dante's work, but it is clear that Giovanni, like Dante, is being instructed and tested, that he too has a chance of winning a high and holy faith through Beatrice. Old Dame Lisabetta's initial outburst, though apparently cliché-ridden, really furnishes a highly significant clue to the action: "*Holy Virgin,* signor!" she cries. "Do you find this old mansion gloomy? *For the love of Heaven,* then, put your head out of the window."

Thus the real question of the story is whether Giovanni has the ability to attain and hold a religious faith or heavenly love against the challenge of materialistic skepticism. His qualifications for this test are by no means outstanding. Remarkably handsome and somewhat superficial, he has "a quick fancy and an ardent southern temperament." Constitutionally, he resembles his father's old friend Baglioni. Yet, as Hawthorne wrote in the introductory sketch to *Mosses from an Old Manse,* "The earthliest human soul has an infinite spiritual capacity" (II, 16), and Giovanni is potentially capable of transforming his ardent earthly passion into something much nobler.

As we might expect from the dualism of Giovanni and the others, the action in the story consists of an alternation of moods, a wavering, one might say, between salvation and damnation. Giovanni vacillates between hope and dread, faith and doubt; and the intermixture of these conflicting emotions makes the garden a veritable hell for him. In this connection, it is worth recalling Hawthorne's devotion to Bunyan. The episode in *Pilgrim's Progress* that most profoundly impressed him was the one in which the shepherds of the Delectable Mountains showed Christian first the byway to hell and then the perspective glass through which could be seen the gates of the Celestial City. Through the byway to hell passed hypocrites, blasphemers, and liars. Hawthorne referred to this byway in describing Ethan Brand's lime kiln: "It resembled nothing so much as *the private entrance* to the infernal regions, which the shepherds of the Delectable Mountains were accustomed to show to pilgrims."[5] Giovanni is led into Rappaccini's garden through a "private entrance" —a point deliberately emphasized by repetition. But the garden, as we have already suggested, is like the Hall of Fantasy in being an inner world incorporating both hell and heaven. The hall has in its observatory "that wonderful perspective glass, through which the shepherds of the Delectable Mountains showed Christian the far-off gleam of the Celestial City. The eye of Faith still loves to gaze through it." Rappaccini's garden has no such glass, but it does have the "pure whiteness of Beatrice's image," if Giovanni will but have faith in it. Thus Hawthorne has fashioned this garden to include, among other things, what he considered "the most awful truth in Bunyan's book of such,—from the very gate of heaven there is a by-way to the pit" (V, 595).

Giovanni's failure to sustain a high faith results from his quite understandable but nonetheless unfortunate reliance upon his senses as the ultimate criterion of truth. Each of the five senses is involved. His vision would seem to be accurate enough to distinguish appearance from reality. But his first glimpse of Beatrice occurs in the deceptive shadows of late afternoon, "and Giovanni, at his lofty window, rubbed his eyes, and almost doubted whether it were a girl tending her favorite flower, or one sister performing the duties of affection to another." The bright sunlight of the next day restores confidence in his sight; the garden that had seemed so mysterious now looks to be a "real and matter-of-fact affair." After wining and dining with Baglioni, he resumes his vantage point at the lofty window and witnesses Beatrice

[5] This byway is also mentioned in "The Celestial Railroad" (II, 231).

in the act of plucking a blossom from the shrub. Again some doubt is cast upon his vision: "It appeared to Giovanni—but at the distance from which he gazed, he could scarcely have seen anything so minute—it appeared to him, however, that a drop or two of moisture from the broken stem of the flower descended upon the lizard's head." The resultant death of the lizard is unmistakable; so is the subsequent death of the insect. Or is it? At any rate he is bewildered enough to ask, "Have I my senses?"

He has them, all right; there can be no question about that. He hears Beatrice's voice and has a synesthetic reaction; it is "a voice as rich as a tropical sunset . . . which made Giovanni, though he knew not why, think of deep hues of purple or crimson and of perfumes heavily delectable." He gradually comes to inhale the fragrance of the flowers with an eager enjoyment that is a veritable "appetite." Seen in the total pattern of the story, Giovanni's advice to Baglioni has an ironic truth to it: "Odors," he tells the eminent professor, "being a sort of element combined of the sensual and the spiritual, are apt to deceive us. . . . The recollection of a perfume, the bare idea of it, may easily be mistaken for a present reality."

To Baglioni, who is far more a creature of the senses than Giovanni, this kind of talk is nonsense. "My sober imagination does not often play me such tricks," he replies. Were I to fancy any kind of odor, it would be that of some *vile apothecary drug, wherewith my fingers are likely to be imbued.*" Like Peter Hovenden, in "The Artist of the Beautiful," who can understand things better when he can touch them, Baglioni has an imagination that extends about as far as the tips of his fingers. Giovanni, it is true, is forced to curb the grossest of his senses. "Touch it not!" cries Beatrice as he starts to pluck a blossom from the purple shrub. And the same caution is implicit in her stern refusal to permit any physical contact between them. On a few occasions Giovanni is "tempted to overstep the limit," but she effectively repels him with a "look of desolate separation."

All Giovanni's sense impressions are incorporated in his "quick fancy." In this story Hawthorne uses the word "fancy" in a special sense: it is the faculty that receives and combines sense impressions. This conception, familiar in medieval and Renaissance literature (as well as in Coleridge and Keats), he probably derived from *Paradise Lost* (V, 100–105):[6]

> . . . know that in the Soul
> Are many lesser Faculties that serve
> Reason as chief; among these Fancy next
> Her office holds; of all external things,
> Which the five watchful Senses represent
> She forms Imaginations, Aery shapes. . . .

We should note, of course, that Hawthorne rejects the Miltonic emphasis upon "reason" as the governing faculty in a well-balanced personality. The psychological conflict in Giovanni lies between fancy and intuition.

The young man's "ardent southern temperament" is at times transmuted into an intuitive faith. Like the innocent pair in "The New Adam and Eve," he and Beatrice find a "reality" in "their mutual glance," which is sharply distinguished from the "dreams and shadows that perplex them everywhere else" (II, 281). Giovanni hopes to find in her "full gaze the mystery which he deemed the riddle of his own existence." Her childlike innocence and purity make him feel more like a brother than lover: "He seemed to gaze through the beautiful girl's eyes into her transparent soul, and felt no more doubt or fear. . . . Her spirit gushed before him

[6] Frank Davidson noted this parallel in "Hawthorne's Hive of Honey," *Modern Language Notes,* LXI (January, 1946), 14–21.

like a fresh rill that was just catching its first glimpse of the sunlight." Even at the very moment when he seems to have conclusive proof of her corruption, Giovanni may, like Dante, see God mirrored in the eyes of Beatrice. He recalls "the delicate and benign power of her feminine nature, which had so often enveloped him in a *religious calm;* recollections of many a *holy* and passionate outgush of her heart, when the pure fountain had been unsealed from its depths and made visible in its transparency to his *mental eye.*"

The superiority of intuition over "fancy," or sense impressions, is explicitly stated more than once in the story. Beatrice tells Giovanni: "Forget whatever you may have fancied in regard to me. If true to the outward sense, still it may be false in its essence; but the words of Beatrice Rappaccini's lips are true from the depths of the heart outward. Those you may believe." The sentiments of Beatrice are, of course, open to suspicion, even though we are told that, as she uttered these words, "A fervor glowed in her whole aspect, and beamed upon Giovanni's consciousness like the light of truth itself." But there is no reason to question Hawthorne's comment, one that in the complex context of the story he has earned the right to interject: "There is something truer and more real than what we can see with the eyes and touch with the fingers."

Giovanni fails to grasp this higher truth. The best comment on his failure can be found in one of Hawthorne's letters: "What delusion can be more lamentable and mischievous," he wrote to Sophia in 1841, "than to mistake the physical and material for the spiritual? What so miserable as to lose the soul's true, though hidden, knowledge and consciousness of heaven in the mist of an earth-born vision?"[7] Giovanni's love

---

[7] In this letter Hawthorne referred specifically to the claims of the mesmerists.

HAWTHORNE'S TRAGIC VISION

grows "thin and faint as the morning mist"; he is overcome by an "earthly illusion" that casts a "mist of evil" over Beatrice. He is incapable of a "high faith" in the "real Beatrice," the "heavenly angel." The person who makes his failure certain is Baglioni. When Peter Hovenden by his very presence destroys Owen Warland's ideal, the young artist calls him his "evil spirit." Giovanni is no Warland, but whatever idealism he possesses is destroyed by the demoniac Baglioni. The professor determines to bring Beatrice "within the limits of ordinary nature"; he places Giovanni's love on the same level as Cellini's amorous adventures. "Behold this silver vase! It was wrought by the hands of Benvenuto Cellini, and is well worthy to be a love gift to the fairest dame in Italy." The vase itself may well be an ominous token, for Cellini informs us in his *Autobiography* that he first made these little silver vases for a clever surgeon, Maestro Giacomo da Carpi. "He was a person of great sagacity," but "all the patients he had treated grew so ill that they were a hundred times worse off than before he came."[8]

Baglioni withdraws, "leaving what he had said to produce its effect upon the young man's mind." Giovanni heeds him, and as a result his spirit is "incapable of sustaining itself at the height to which the early enthusiasm of passion had exalted it; he fell down grovelling among earthly doubts, and defiled therewith the pure whiteness of Beatrice's image. Not that he gave her up; he did but distrust." In his doubt and indecision, Giovanni determines to test Beatrice. It is, of

[8] *The Autobiography of Benvenuto Cellini,* trans. John A. Symonds (Modern Library Series, Random House, New York, 1927), p. 54. For further evidence that Hawthorne was familiar with Cellini's memoirs, see the allusion in "The Virtuoso's Collection" (II, 550). It seems very probable that Hawthorne obtained the names Lisabetta, Guasconti, and Baglioni from Cellini's book; and Dr. Giacomo Rappaccini may well be his combination of the names of the surgeon Giacomo and Raffaelo Lapaccini.

course, a crude test, based upon his senses: "If he could but witness, *at the distance of a few paces,* the sudden blight of one fresh and healthful flower in Beatrice's hand, there would be no room for further question." Giovanni, the exact opposite of Aylmer, has been "guilty of treason to holy love by degrading its perfect idea to the level of the actual" (II, 65).

That Giovanni's love might have risen to religious faith is made plain in his bitterly sarcastic renunciation of it: "Yes, yes; let us pray! Let us to church and dip our fingers in the holy water at the portal!" Rejecting faith in Beatrice, he worships instead the false fruits of Baglioni's materialism. The antidote he offers Beatrice is, Giovanni asserts, "almost *divine* in its efficacy. . . . It is distilled of *blessed* herbs. Shall we not quaff it together, and thus be purified from evil?" What he suggests is that they transcend human limitations and become Godlike; in effect, he is repeating the original temptation in Eden. But the poison in Beatrice, like the birthmark on Georgiana's cheek, cannot be erased except in death. Hawthorne does not need to tell us what would have happened had Giovanni drunk the antidote; the implication is clear enough in Beatrice's last words: "Farewell, Giovanni! Thy words of hatred are like lead within my heart. . . . Oh, was there not, from the first, more poison in thy nature than in mine?"

The central theme of the story can be stated simply enough. The inner world of human experience is a complex and ambiguous mixture of good and evil—the evil here taking shape in the two extremes of intellectual pride and gross materialism. The sheer complexity of such experience sorely tempts us to indulge in crude, quantitative tests—proofs of virtue that can be tested by the senses. But there is no more monstrous delusion than to abandon all idealistic faith in favor of materialistic skepticism. Or, to put it more concretely, what baffles Giovanni is the ambiguity of Beatrice. He would like to possess her physically, or he would be content with her as a pure ideal; but he cannot grasp the fact that she offers both sin and eventual redemption. Such a statement, it is true, fails to sum up "Rappaccini's Daughter," just as the rigid method of analysis inadequately represents the fluid life of Hawthorne's story. From an ordinary point of view, Beatrice *is* poisonous and Giovanni is right in wondering "what evil thing stung him."[9] Yet from an extraordinary point of view, she is a religious ideal and Baglioni is a destructive blasphemer. The two attitudes coexist in the story: the reader naturally leans toward the former, but Hawthorne deliberately counteracts this tendency by emphasizing the latter. The result is a rich irony that this prosaic commentary can but clumsily indicate.

We may conclude by suggesting two further literary associations that form part of the irony. Some reminiscences of Dante, Bunyan, and Milton have already been mentioned. But the influence of Milton is by no means a simple carryover. Hawthorne, writing "Rappaccini's Daughter" during his idyllic married life at the Old Manse, could not fully accept Milton's version of Eve's part in the Fall. With characteristic chivalry he transferred minor bits of Eve's original role to Adam, as he playfully did in "The New Adam and Eve" (II, 293). It is not simply that Giovanni has Eve's golden ringlets and extraordinary beauty; he has her vanity as well. Just as Eve in *Paradise Lost* was pleased by her image in the pool, so Giovanni, at a crucial moment, "failed not to look at his figure in the mirror,—a vanity to be expected in a beautiful young man, yet, as displaying itself at that troubled

[9] Giovanni's comparison of Beatrice to a serpent reminds us of Adam's harsh rebuff of Eve: "Out of my sight, thou Serpent" (*Paradise Lost*, X, 867). Hawthorne's phrase "mist of evil," cited above, may be a reminiscence of Satan's method of entering Eden.

The Ambiguity of Beatrice

and feverish moment, the token of a certain shallowness of feeling and insincerity of character." It is Beatrice who warns him away from the purple shrub—the fruit of her father's "fatal science"; it is Giovanni who tempts her with the equally fatal antidote. She accepts, like Milton's Adam, "not deceiv'd." And this reversal of traditional roles extends beyond Milton back to Dante again. As Giovanni mistakes heavenly for earthly love, so Beatrice errs in considering him heaven-sent (II, 143), an "image" to be kept in her heart. This irony reaches its height with Giovanni's strikingly imperceptive hope of "*leading* Beatrice, the *redeemed* Beatrice, by the hand."

It need not be emphasized that the distinction between heavenly and earthly love is a key element not only in Raphael's warning to Adam (*Paradise Lost*, VIII, 521–643) but also in the Palmer's instruction to Sir Guyon in Book II of *The Faerie Queene*. There are other Spenserian parallels in the story (Archimago, as Randall Stewart has suggested,[10] may have influenced Hawthorne's characterization of Rappaccini), but I should like to concentrate on one final detail. Beatrice is carefully associated with an "antique sculptured portal." She enters and leaves the garden through this portal; she vanishes beneath it; it is mentioned six times in the story. Readers of Spenser will recall a well-known "sculptured portal," the carved ivory gate to the Bower of Bliss (II, xii, 44):

> Yt framed was of precious yvory
> That seemd a worke of admirable wit;
> And therin all the famous history
> of Iason and Medaea was ywrit;
> Her mighty charmes, her furious loving fit,

[10] "Hawthorne and The Faerie Queen," *Philological Quarterly*, XII (April, 1933), 196–206.

> His goodly conquest of the golden fleece,
> His falsed faith, and love too lightly flit,
> The wondred *Argo,* which in venturous peece
> First through the Euxine seas bore all the flowr of *Greece.*

The story of Jason is somewhat similar to that of Giovanni, in that it is one of "falsed faith, and love too lightly flit"; and the parallel between Medea and both Acrasia and Beatrice is obvious.[11] But in the story Giovanni himself, though in bitter scorn, associates the portal with the church—with prayer, holy water, and religious faith. In this one detail, as elsewhere in "Rappaccini's Daughter," literary reminiscences heighten the fascinating ambiguity of Beatrice.

The structure of the story reinforces our statement of its theme. There is a house and a garden, an outer and an inner world. In the beginning we see Giovanni's fair head framed by the window. He is somewhat homesick but not yet bewildered by the ambiguities and intricacies of the inner world. The masterly ending does more than provide a pleasing symmetry. We see the window again; but the face of Giovanni has been supplanted—obliterated, one might say—by the triumphant countenance of Baglioni, who has never entered the inner world. His loud voice confirms the triumph of the external, the superficial, the mediocre.

[11] Fogle has suggested the Jason-Medea story as a parallel, though not in connection with the sculptured portal. *Hawthorne's Fiction,* p. 102.

Speculation and Investment

AFTER OUR DETAILED examination of "Rappaccini's Daughter," we may comment more
briefly upon five other stories that deal in different ways with
the same basic issues. "The Celestial Railroad" offers Hawthorne's delightful critique of America's often-repeated
efforts at painless purification. In "Young Goodman Brown"
we find a representative young man who, like Giovanni Guasconti, is baffled and benumbed by the ambiguity of good and
evil he discovers in his Faith. In "The Birthmark," another
effort is made—this time an idealistic one—to transform the
duality of woman into something simple and pure. In "The
Artist of the Beautiful," Hawthorne considers what is gained

and lost when art is substituted for love. And finally in "Ethan Brand" we see the artist as Satan, inverting his vision and simply using the woman as one of many experiments.

The issues involved in these stories may be somewhat arbitrarily comprehended under the two headings "speculation" and "investment." "Speculation" we defined earlier as the masculine function of penetrating into space, rending timeworn structures, gambling on something new. "Investment" encompasses the feminine role of mending and conserving traditional values. If we think of speculation as penetration, these terms have the advantage of applying to economic, sexual, and moral experience in a way that appealed to Hawthorne, as it did to Melville and Thoreau.

The dialectic between speculation and investment may be briefly illustrated by *Moby Dick,* although any brief comment on that book is perhaps an impertinence. The voyage of the *Pequod* is a gamble in which all hands share competitively. Their "lays" vary according to their ability to penetrate the layers of the whale and convert it into oil, and the material conversion is paralleled by their ways of gaining knowledge. The process is one of stripping, penetrating, fasting, and cutting in; but it is also investing, feeding, baptizing, and weaving. Most members of the crew are interested solely in particulars—in particular whales—and their ability to penetrate is limited to physical skill with harpoon and lance. Flask, for instance, the mere vessel containing all the simple heartlessness of unenlightened masculinity, pricks the sore spot in the old diseased whale. Contrasting with the whalers but sharing their limited penetration are the timeworn Usher and the "sub-sub-librarian." The one supplies etymologies, the other "extracts"; both fail to use their knowledge in action, while Flask acts without knowledge.

In Ahab, the captain who knows both cannibals and col-

Speculation and Investment

leges, we see the crippling effect of riveting one's attention upon the universal. Having rended all humane bonds, he binds himself to the devil and dies with his neck in the noose. He can penetrate; he sees right through the "pasteboard masks" of invisible objects, but his error lies in thinking they are merely pasteboard. He feels only contempt for letters or gossipy particulars; he wants the universal whale, and in fixing his gaze upon it he sees it only as evil.

For Ahab, the voyage is the ultimate in unconditional speculation; for Ishmael, the trip is a great investment. Giving up his role as schoolmaster where he lorded it over the schoolboys, he provides the humane and somewhat feminine counterbalance to Ahab's masculinity. He accepts the universal thump; he views the white whale with reverent awe; he puts on the monkey rope, weaves the mat, squeezes the spermacetti, and rejoices in the way the skeleton of the whale is clothed by vines and flowers. Thus he qualifies for the "resurrection" he had yearned for under the counterpane with Queequeg; he unites the particular and the universal in the symbol and the symbolic act; having participated in a spiritual death with Ahab, he is able to wear the wooden coffin-lifebuoy and be rescued by the *Rachel.*

The sexual element in Melville's work has doubtless been overemphasized. In Hawthorne's fiction, where the imagery is more subtle and delicate, it is easy to miss the implications of the staffs and canes carried by his penetrating speculators, and of the ribbons and flowers worn by the women. The most overt allusions occur, as we shall see, in *The House of the Seven Gables,* where the sexual brutality of the Judge is symbolized by his cane and his contribution to agriculture— the Pyncheon bull; in *The Blithedale Romance,* where the abortive sexual relation between Zenobia and Hollingsworth is symbolized in the midnight probing for her body; and in

"Young Goodman Brown." No service would be done to Hawthorne's art by exaggerating the importance of his sexual symbols, but our usual error, as Professor Stewart has pointed out in restoring the text of the *American* and *English Notebooks,* is to think of him as being more genteel than he was.

Hawthorne customarily symbolized the humane qualities of investment in the unobtrusive feminine task of sewing. "There is something extremely pleasant . . . in this peculiarity of needlework," he wrote in *The Marble Faun.* "The slender thread of silk or cotton keeps them [women] united with the small, familiar, gentle interests of life, the continually operating influences of which do so much for the health of the character, and carry off what would otherwise be a dangerous accumulation of morbid sensibility. A vast deal of human sympathy runs along this electric line, stretching from the throne to the wicker chair of the humblest seamstress, and keeping high and low in a species of communion with their kindred beings" (VI, 55–56). Miriam's sewing, as well as the imaginative sympathy of her sketches, typifies a life filled with the rich compassion of womanhood; Zenobia, on the other hand, in competing with men has delegated all her gentler qualities to her stepsister and handmaid, the seamstress Priscilla. It is through her needlework that Hester Prynne knows Pearl and becomes involved with community life; the solitary Hepzibah Pyncheon, however, has fingers "at once inflexible and delicate," which prevent her from sewing. The value of investment may be summed up, then, in the myth of Ariadne, whose thread leads Theseus out of the labyrinth of speculation (IV, 239).

To speculate is to erect a kind of watchtower (*specula*) from which one can gain a detached perspective and "take stock." To invest, on the other hand, is to accept the bond. The ironic parallels between economic and moral life are neatly worked out in Hawthorne's satirical sketch "The Celestial Railroad." Seizing upon the railroad as a symbol of the greatest speculative enterprise in America and equating it with the progressive morality and religion of his time, Hawthorne measures them both against John Bunyan's "road-book." Guided by Mr. Smooth-It-Away, who personifies the various insidious leveling forces operating in Hawthorne's time and who is one of the largest stockholders in the railroad, the narrator decides to gratify his "liberal" curiosity by entraining for a quick and painless trip to the Celestial City. The famous Slough of Despond has been shakily paved over by rationalistic tracts, the strait gate has been widened, the burdens have been stowed in the baggage car, and the conversation pleasantly concerns the news of the day.

The details of Hawthorne's satire may be directly related to the Unitarian movement. But they apply equally well to modern quests for peaceful purification. At Vanity Fair, "If a customer wished to renew his stock of youth the dealers offered him a set of false teeth and an auburn wig; if he demanded peace of mind, they recommended opium or a brandy bottle." Hawthorne clearly anticipated other modern shortcuts, such as courses in mass communication where "any man may acquire an omnigenous erudition without the trouble of learning to read."

Hawthorne's chief concern was with the questionable moral character of the "speculations." In a passage that Melville marked, Hawthorne called attention to a machine for "the wholesale manufacture of individual morality. This excellent result is effected by societies for all manner of virtuous purposes, with which a man has merely to connect himself, throwing, as it were, his quota of virtue into the common stock, and the president and directors will take care that the aggregate amount be well applied." Despite all these and

other "wonderful improvements in ethics, religion, and literature," individuals have a way of vanishing from Vanity Fair,
presumably having been transported to the Dark Valley of
the Shadow of Death. Amid all this speculation, no investment takes place. One young man squanders most of his
inheritance for the purchase of diseases and finally spends all
the rest for "a heavy lot of repentance and a suit of rags." The
clothing of the travelers, safely stowed in the baggage car,
consists of "a great variety of favorite Habits, which we
trusted would not be out of fashion even in the polite circles
of the Celestial City."

As Hawthorne was to point out more somberly in *The
Blithedale Romance*, the weakness in the philosophy of technological and intellectual uplift is that it confuses penetration in space with moral insight. Seeking salvation in endless
motion, the modern mechanized pilgrims discover, ironically
enough, that their vehicle lacks substance and efficiency. The
whole concern is "a bubble," the railroad will never get beyond the limits of Vanity Fair, and without roots the enterprise lacks body. No "act of incorporation" will ever be issued
by the Lord of the Celestial City for this railroad, "and unless
that be obtained, no passenger can ever hope to enter his
dominion. Wherefore every man who buys a ticket must lay
his account with losing the purchase money, which is the
value of his own soul."

With our categories of speculation and investment established, we are now ready to confront the devil's staff and the
pink ribbon of "Young Goodman Brown." One of the world's
great short stories, it has prompted considerable critical comment. Fogle has very effectively shown how ambiguity of
meaning and clarity of technique combine in the art of the

story, and F. O. Matthiessen praised it highly, though he was
troubled by the pink ribbons.[1] As I shall try to demonstrate,
the ribbons lead to that aspect of the story which is usually
missed—the fact that Faith's ambiguity is the ambiguity of
womanhood and that the dark night in the forest is essentially
a sexual experience, though it is also much more.

Young Goodman Brown, whose name indicates his kinship
with Goody Cloyse and Deacon Gookin—that is, his role as
Everyman—seems destined to spend a night in the forest,
just as his wife's pink ribbons seem to be part of her. In the
town daylight his Faith is simple and innocuous. "She's a
blessed angel on earth; and after this one night I'll cling to
her skirts and follow her to heaven," he says. But this one
night, this one involvement with the ambiguity of good and
evil, will so shatter him that his dying hour will be gloom.
For Faith and her pink ribbon, so pure in the sunlight, are
fiendish at night. There is just a faint suggestion of the transition at sunset, when Faith whispers softly to Brown, "tarry
with me."

Faith, like Beatrice Rappaccini, is both pure and poisonous,
saint and sinner. She *is* in the forest that night, and the pink
ribbons blend with the serpentine staff in what becomes a
fiery orgy of lust. In marrying her, Brown has been introduced
to a devilish traveler who strongly resembles his father. The
most conspicuous thing about this stranger is his wriggling
staff, which suggests the knowledge of the serpent—and also
serves as a means of penetrating into space.

One of the guests who will attend the midnight ceremonies
is Goody Cloyse. She has lost her broomstick—"and that, too,
when I was all anointed with the juice of smallage, and
cinquefoil, and wolf's bane"—but she borrows the devil's

[1] Fogle, *Hawthorne's Fiction*, pp. 15–32; Matthiessen, *American Renaissance*, pp. 282–84.

staff to help her speed onward. "They tell me there is a nice young man to be taken into communion tonight," she cackles. Brown balks at going further; the devil lends him a staff and disappears into the gloom. Next the voices of two riders are heard. As one stops to pluck a switch, the voices become more distinct and seem to belong to Deacon Gookin and the minister. "There is a goodly young woman to be taken into communion," announces the deacon. And his lecherous old companion makes this double-edged rejoinder: "Spur up, or we shall be late. Nothing can be done, you know, until I get on the ground."

Almost everything in the forest scene suggests that the communion of sinners is essentially sexual and that Brown qualifies for it by his marriage. Having witnessed the pink ribbon impaled upon the branch of a tree, Brown seizes the devil's staff and speeds toward the sounds of the gathering multitude. The details of the setting subtly reveal further images of penetration and investment:

At one extremity of an open space, hemmed in by the dark wall of the forest, arose a rock, bearing some rude, natural resemblance either to an altar or a pulpit, and surrounded by four blazing pines, their tops aflame, their stems untouched, like candles at an evening meeting. The mass of foliage that had overgrown the summit of the rock was all on fire, blazing high into the night and fitfully illuminating the whole field. Each pendant twig and leafy festoon was in a blaze.

The ceremony is a magnificent blending of folklore and superstition, containing elements of the Black Mass and the witch sabbath. It is also a dark marriage, in which Brown and Faith are taken into communion with their race. The "one stain of guilt," the "deep mystery of sin," is set forth

Speculation and Investment

in the crimes of sexual passion described by the devil. He tells how

hoary-bearded elders of the church have whispered wanton words to the young maids of their households; how many a woman, eager for widow's weeds, has given her husband a drink at bedtime and let him sleep his last sleep in her bosom; how beardless youths have made haste to inherit their fathers' wealth; and how fair damsels—blush not, sweet ones—have dug little graves in the garden, and bidden me, the sole guest to an infant's funeral.

The whole affair, of course, may well have been a dream, but, whether dream or no, the ultimate effect on Brown is the same. "Truth," as Hawthorne wrote in "The Birthmark," "often finds its way to the mind close muffled in robes of sleep" (II, 52).

One effect of "marriage"—whether the wedding is of man and woman or a complete involvement with an art or a religion—is the shock of recognizing the reality of the past. The tapestry conserving the vital patterns of man's limitations and potentialities as expressed in myth, legend, and superstition gradually unfolds, and the young man becomes painfully aware of his cultural and familial parentage. For Brown the shocks are too much to bear. He sees the devil in his father's shape; he hears him say, "I helped your grandfather, the constable, when he lashed the Quaker woman so smartly through the streets of Salem; and it was I that brought your father a pitch-pine knot, kindled at my own heart, to set fire to an Indian village." Brown is also stupefied by the vision of evil that seems to infest all the foundations of church and state.

Brown's dying hour is gloom, then, because he fails to attain a tragic vision, a perspective broad enough and deep enough to see the dark night as an essential part of human experience, but a part that may prelude a new and richer dawn. Returning from the forest, he sees "Faith, with the pink ribbons, gazing anxiously forth, and bursting into such joy at the sight of him that she skipped along the street and almost kissed her husband before the whole village." But Brown, like Giovanni, is unable to grasp this higher faith.

While Young Goodman Brown is overwhelmed by the vision of evil, Aylmer in "The Birthmark" refuses to recognize its deep-rooted reality. For him the earthly stain can be expunged by the alchemy of science; his faith rests in man's ability to speculate, to penetrate by repeated experiments. The story takes place during the late eighteenth century, "in those days when the comparatively recent discovery of electricity and other kindred mysteries of Nature seemed to open paths into the region of miracle" (II, 47). The setting is appropriate, for this was the period when the Romantic challenge to the mathematical, mechanical world view was stimulated by Galvani's experiments in Italy. As Coleridge pointed out in his lecture to a London audience in 1819:[2]

From the time of Kepler to Newton, and from that to Hartley, not only all things in external nature, but the subtlest mysteries of life and organization, even of the intellect and moral being, were conjured within the magic circle of mathematical formality. But now a light was struck by the discovery of electricity, and in every sense of the word . . . it may be affirmed to have electrified the whole form of natural philosophy.

[2] See Roy R. Male, "Hawthorne and the Concept of Sympathy," *Publications of the Modern Language Association*, LXVIII (March, 1953), 138–49.

Speculation and Investment

Aylmer is thus placed in a period when the age-old question of the secret of life again became acute as the physiological doctrines advanced by the Scotsman John Brown and the Swiss Albrecht von Haller seemed to culminate in Galvani's observation of the twitching frogs' legs. After Brown and Haller had theoretically reduced the manifold complications of animation to the irritability of muscles and the sensibility of nerves, the conflict between mechanism and vitalism took on an impassioned fervor, revolving around such vague concepts as "nervous fluid," "vital force," and "principle of life." Therefore when in 1786 Galvani successfully brought about artificial movements in dead organic matter, there were many who believed that the basic principle of life was close to revelation and that the gap between mind and matter could be bridged.

As a forward-looking scientist of his time, Aylmer owns an electrical machine as part of his equipment for conversion. His faith in this equipment provides one of the lesser ironies of the story, for when he tells Georgiana that her birthmark "shocks" him, she retorts, "You cannot love what shocks you." Her rejoinder is quite to the point: Aylmer has an antidote for those shocks of recognition which so benumbed Goodman Brown and Giovanni Guasconti—his electrical machine and kindred gadgets. In short, Aylmer has confused the province of science with that of religion and morality.

Robert B. Heilman's extremely effective discussion shows how the confusion of science and religion reveals itself in the language patterns of the story.[3] The scientists are called "votaries"; their studies are "mysteries"; Aylmer becomes virtually the God of the new religion of science. He has sub-

[3] "Hawthorne's 'The Birthmark': Science as Religion," *South Atlantic Quarterly*, LXVIII (October, 1949), 575–83.

HAWTHORNE'S TRAGIC VISION

verted the old creed; Aminadab, a high priest in the Bible, has been transformed into his laboratory assistant.[4] As Heilman rightly remarks, Aylmer's tragedy "is that he lacks the tragic sense; he is, we may say, a characteristic modern, the exponent of an age which has deified science and regards it as an irresistibly utopianizing force. His tragic flaw is to fail to see the tragic flaw of humanity."

Aylmer is no mere technologist; he perceives the dangers of his premises. But this idealistic strain makes him all the more dangerous. It enables him to convert his wife to the enterprise so that Georgiana becomes not a passive victim but a fascinated participant in his quest for scientific purification. The major irony in the story lies in the way they exaggerate the Original Sin in their very attempt to avoid it. Aylmer proudly takes over the feminine role of investment; he hangs the walls of the boudoir with gorgeous curtains that "shut in the scene from infinite space," and he replaces the sunlight with perfumed lamps.

Conversely, Georgiana becomes fascinated by the fruit of Aylmer's knowledge. Subject to "certain physical influences, either breathed in with the fragrant air or taken with her food," she resembles Eve listening to the Serpent describe "the Cure of All." Eve, we recall, had been tempted by Satan's glowing recollection of his "speculations high or deep." Georgiana, in her growing, inverted pride, turns over the volumes of Aylmer's scientific library, perusing the speculations of Albertus Magnus, Cornelius Agrippa, and Paracelsus. As she reads the records of Aylmer's own experiments, she loves him more than ever, "but with less entire dependence on his judgment than heretofore." Thus she moves from the "fantastic elegance" of her boudoir, overdecorated by Aylmer,

[4] See William R. Thompson, "Aminadab in Hawthorne's 'The Birthmark,'" *Modern Language Notes* (June, 1955), 413–15.

Speculation and Investment

to the naked walls, brick pavements, and gaseous odors of his laboratory, complete with its "distilling apparatus." In this Eden of the present world, as in Rappaccini's garden, all the values represented in womanhood are distilled right out of existence.

Art comes much closer than science to providing a detour to the Celestial City. But it, too, has its limitations and its dangers. The problem of the ideal artist, as Hawthorne views it in "The Artist of the Beautiful," is that he must wed a masculine strength and experimental ability with a feminine ingenuity and imaginative sympathy in order to conceive a living work of art. In a passage that Melville heavily marked, Hawthorne wrote, "It is requisite for the ideal artist to possess a force of character that seems hardly compatible with its delicacy; he must keep his faith in himself while the incredulous world assails him with its utter disbelief" (II, 512). This reconciliation of opposites within himself typifies the whole artistic process.

Warland's work unites clock time with seasonal time (duration) in eternity; he fuses nature and spirit in art. Thus the life of his artistic butterfly is a kind of "magnetism." It is difficult to avoid crudity in discussing this "magnetism"; as Coleridge noted in his "Theory of Life," we tend to think of various electromagnetic devices. But Warland does not refer to the physical phenomenon; he has rejected the mechanical contrivances of others as "mere impositions." What he means is that his work of art has become vital through a typically magnetic reconciliation of opposites, the major poles being spirit and matter. This has been possible only because he has instilled within his work his own intellect, imagination, and sensibility, his own periods of "torpid slumber" and rebirth, his rhythmic oscillation between the tense, isolated nights of artistic creation and his aimless wanderings in woods and fields.

Warland's art does "beat all nature," as Danforth's cliché indicates. But in wedding his art instead of the woman he loses in strength what he gains in refinement. There are two Annie Hovendens: the "ordinary woman" who marries Danforth and gives birth to a new version of Peter Hovenden, and the Annie who has been invested with angelic qualities by Warland's "inward vision." The ideal fashioned by Warland's imagination might conceivably have existed, and with his adoration she might have inspired a worthier art. But since he confined "the career of his passion" to his "artist's imagination," this possibility remains only conjectural.

Certainly the crucial scene, in which Annie comes to the artist's workshop, casts doubt upon any finer qualities she might have possessed. Here again we notice that each concrete object in the story is carefully chosen. Annie Hovenden comes to the artist equipped with the symbols of her position in the warm fireside circle of humanity—thimble and needle. As he glances at the damaged thimble, Owen seizes eagerly upon the idea that this girl, who is perceptive enough to grasp his aim of "putting spirit into machinery," might be able to offer him companionship in his lonely toil. But her warm earthy sympathy is irreconcilable with his quest for the ideal; it takes but a touch from the point of her needle to destroy his project. This is the exact converse of the situation in "The Birthmark," where Aylmer's quest for a scientific ideal destroys Georgiana.

Even though the concrete object of his art is crushed by the child of strength, Warland derives consolation, however frail it may seem, from the knowledge that he has achieved his ideal aim. He has attained it, furthermore, without distorting himself or violating the wholeness of others. But as Fogle has pointed out, this success is partly due to the slightness of his art and its remoteness from human life. The butterfly does not penetrate even the surface of human existence; it must remain aloof or it is destroyed. Had Warland wrestled with massive materials, the outcome might have been quite different.

In "Ethan Brand" we see what that outcome might have been. For Brand, too, is an artist, but his art involves the most weighty of all matters, the problem of evil. Like Satan's, his speculations have been high and deep; like Ahab, Brand has a "sense of evil so inflexible, so adamant in its refusal to admit the not less reducible fact of existent good that it is perilously close to a love of evil, a queer pact with the devil."[5] In penetrating the superficial, Brand becomes transfixed by the vision of evil and ultimately embraces its destructive power.

One source of the story's intensity can be found in Hawthorne's account of his own creative processes. The fire possessed a special poignancy for Hawthorne, since it consumed much of his apprentice writing. In the preface to *A Wonder-Book for Boys and Girls* he referred to the difficulty of rendering legends malleable in his "intellectual furnace." With this metaphor in mind, Brand can readily be seen as artist. Both he and Bartram are lime-burners, but Bartram calls it a "business," Brand a "craft"; Bartram turns away from the insufferable glare of the furnace, while Brand pro-

[5] This is R. W. B. Lewis' description of one of the alternatives seen by Ishmael in "The Try-Works." *The American Adam,* p. 132.

jects his dark thoughts into its intense glow. For him, the craft of conversion has been a lonely and "intensely thoughtful occupation."

But obviously, "Ethan Brand" is not a self-portrait, nor is it simply an exorcising of Hawthorne's fears about himself and his occupation. It is a story about two ways of life, one of them incomplete and the other prematurely completed. The first is an untempered, uninformed comic vision, typified by the minor characters. Almost everyone in the story except Brand is a performer of some kind, seeking a circus atmosphere: Bartram, the "clown"; Lawyer Giles, who had a great vogue in his day; the stage agent, famed as a dry wit; the doctor, a village medicine man; Esther, who had gone off with the circus and performed marvelous feats on the tightrope; the itinerant showman with his diorama; the self-impelled, self-pursuing dog; even the stage-driver who sounds his horn/ One exhibition follows another in a ritualistic quest for laughter, as the jolly fellows from the tavern and the merry youths from the town gather in a crowd to observe first Ethan Brand, then the Wandering Jew, and finally the "canine performer." They seek amusement, but when they hear Brand's laughter they are silenced by its spine-chilling horror. It is like Hawthorne's grim interjection in "The Maypole of Merry Mount," which abruptly cuts through the systematic gaiety of the silken colonists: "But did the dead man laugh?"

Contrasted to the obsessive youthfulness of the townspeople is the premature old age of Brand's absorption with sin. Instead of the discrete fragments to which their perception is limited, he has melted all his thoughts and welded them into one idea. He has achieved unity at the cost of fanatic distortion; his completed circle is self-centered and self-constricting. In repeating Satan's desire for ultimate penetration, he has followed his prototype by callously using the woman as an experiment in evil. His might be called the "unoriginal sin" in the sense that it originates nothing: the fruit of his life's labor is simply the unpardonable sin. Thus Brand has precipitately hardened his categories and his heart; in penetrating, he himself is reduced to an antique skeleton whose "relics" are finally crumbled into "fragments" by the oafish Bartram.

Brand's career may be summed up in the house imagery that runs as a minor strain throughout the story. It begins with little Joe at play, building houses with "scattered fragments of marble"; it ends with Brand finding his home at the bottom of the kiln. Originally Brand viewed the heart of man with reverence, considering it a sacred temple. In pursuing his studies he progressed far beyond Bartram's state of living in a hut, little better than an animal stooped close to the ground. And his self-education carried him far beyond the jolly fellows of the tavern. But in his isolated pride he lost "the key of holy sympathy"; he found a home in the tower instead of the temple. As Bartram says, "The man's head is turned." He stands erect on the tower and looks down into the flames with the inverted vision of Satan.

In the two views of life we have summarized, there may be a clue to one of the most puzzling problems raised by the story. Why did Hawthorne subtitle it "A Chapter from an Abortive Romance" and make seemingly careless allusions to an unfinished longer work? He says, "as we have seen," when we have not; he refers to "the Esther of our tale" and we wonder, "What tale?" Even if we assume that a longer romance existed, why did Hawthorne, who was ordinarily scrupulous about the effect of each expression, fail to spend a few minutes making the necessary deletions before he published the story in the *Dollar Magazine*?

The answer, I think, lies in the images and meaning of the story, for, as we have observed, it deals with fragmentation and premature unity. It might be summarized as follows: Man's knowledge is necessarily incomplete and fragmentary. His noblest impulses urge him to transform these particles into a unified structure, and if he does not make this effort he remains little better than an animal. But if he does realize a single unified view and proudly insist upon it, his "one idea" inevitably becomes a crazy distortion. Now we know that Hawthorne often felt himself perilously close to Ethan Brand's predicament. Absorbed in his one idea that the fires of sin and suffering were necessary for moral purification, projecting his own artistic ideas into the fireplace at night, isolated in his craft, he knew Brand intimately. Thus allusions to an unfinished work and the fragments from it that he deliberately left in the story may well be a kind of private reassurance that he had kept his flexibility and balance, that, unlike Brand, he had retained a dual vision of life and would not be unseated by the vision of evil.

This suggestion does not preclude one's impression that in "Ethan Brand" Hawthorne was moving toward a longer work. In this connection one other point ought to be clarified—the allegorical identity of the Wandering Jew. When Brand is confronted by the maimed human beings of the tavern, he doubts for a moment that he is the unpardonable sinner. But old Humphrey's reference to Esther, whom Brand wasted in his experiments, convinces him of his guilt. To corroborate this, his guilt now appears on the scene. In "Fancy's Show Box," Hawthorne had suggested that guilt might be imagined in the form of "an itinerant showman, with a box of pictures on her back" (I, 251). With a change in gender, here is the germ of the old German Jew who confronts Ethan Brand after the mention of Esther's name. Like the Virtuoso in "A

Speculation and Investment

Virtuoso's Collection," he has been everywhere, though men prefer not to recognize him. But Brand knows him when he sees himself reflected in the diorama. We will see more of this image of guilt, for he reappears in various guises throughout Hawthorne's full-length romances.

vi —

The Tongue of Flame:
The Scarlet Letter

I CONSIDER *The Scarlet Letter* the most intensely moving and the most beautifully composed work in American fiction. No other book, to use D. H. Lawrence's words, is so deep, so dual, and so complete.[1] It never fails to interest even those uninitiated readers who approach it, as they say, "just for the story." For the reader who seeks something more than an interesting narrative, there is "surface beneath surface, to an immeasurable depth" (VII, 132).

[1] *Studies in Classic American Literature,* p. 111. Lawrence refers only to Hawthorne's fiction in this judgment.

The Tongue of Flame: The Scarlet Letter

This is Hawthorne's comment about Shakespeare's plays, but it applies equally well to his own masterpiece.

The critic faces two major difficulties in discussing the book. Its plot is so lucid that almost every reader thinks he already knows what *The Scarlet Letter* is about. Thus what seem to be the most obvious symbols—Pearl, Roger Chillingworth, the letter itself—are actually the most often misunderstood. Second, the book's texture is so tightly interwoven that any formal or categorical exposition seems fated to produce distortion. To some extent this is true in any analysis of a successful literary work. But the extraordinary unity of *The Scarlet Letter* makes separation of its elements particularly painful.

As it is usually interpreted, the book is said to deal with the consequences of sin upon three individuals. A symmetrical pattern is discerned in which Hester Prynne is the openly repentant sinner, Arthur Dimmesdale the half-repentant sinner, and Roger Chillingworth the unrepentant sinner.[2] Pearl is to be understood as the symbol of the sin, the living embodiment of the scarlet letter. Beyond this point there is less critical agreement—in fact, there is very little agreement at all. Most critics think *The Scarlet Letter* is essentially Hester Prynne's story, but a few, most notably Henry James, have felt that Dimmesdale is really more important. The moral significance of the action has been heatedly argued, with opinions ranging from fervent glorification of Hester's "triumph" as an instance of *felix culpa* to orthodox satisfaction at the inexorable punishment meted out to the sinners.[3]

This widespread disagreement among critics has been taken as a tribute to the richness of the book. Doubtless the

[2] See Yvor Winters, *Maule's Curse* (New Directions, New York, 1938), p. 16.

[3] These conflicting views are summarized by Frederic I. Carpenter, "Scarlet A Minus," *College English,* V (January, 1944), 173–80.

meaning of any work of art that plumbs the mysteries of human life will be subject to endless debate. Yet, if the book is artistically successful, there ought to be limits to the debate; if the work's broad structure is not clear, we deal not with ambiguity and paradox but with confusion. Now if any work of fiction immediately impresses the reader as having a clean classic structure it is *The Scarlet Letter*, with its symmetrical pillory scenes, its subtle contrasts and massive ironies. Yet even here we find total disagreement. In one of the best interpretations of the book, John C. Gerber has cogently argued that it divides into four unequal parts: In Part I (Chapters I to VIII) it is the community that instigates the action; in Part II (Chapters IX to XII) it is Chillingworth; in Part III (Chapters XIII to XIX), it is Hester; and in Part IV (Chapters XX to XXIV), it is Dimmesdale. Newton Arvin has more tentatively suggested that there are eight scenes that can be grouped into the conventional five acts of a play. Anne Marie MacNamara, who agrees with Henry James that *The Scarlet Letter* is Dimmesdale's story, divides his spiritual growth into four stages: preparation (Chapters I to XVI); communication (Chapters XVII to XIX); transformation (Chapters XX to XXII); and revelation (Chapter XXIII).[4]

None of these divergent outlines can be absolutely rejected; each has a partial validity. The same may be said of the initial premise upon which the conventional interpretations are based—that the book concerns the effects of sin upon the three individuals. This reading is unquestionably accurate as

[4] John C. Gerber, "Form and Content in *The Scarlet Letter*," *New England Quarterly*, XVII (March, 1944), 25–55; Newton Arvin, ed., *The Scarlet Letter* (Modern Classics Series, Harper & Brothers, New York, 1950), p. xii; Anne Marie MacNamara, "'The Character of Flame': The Function of Pearl in *The Scarlet Letter*," *American Literature*, XXVII (January, 1956), 537–53. I am indebted to Miss MacNamara's article at several points in my interpretation of Dimmesdale's relation to Pearl.

far as it goes, and to encompass something like the full meaning of the book such interpretations as those of Winters, Gerber, and Mark Van Doren should be held in suspension with the version I am about to propose. Fortunately, *The Scarlet Letter* cannot be reduced to any single explication.

Consider, however, some of the questions that the usual reading of the book fails to answer. Why did Hester marry Chillingworth in the first place? Apparently not for money; certainly not for love. Why does Hawthorne spend so much space on Pearl and on the letter if they are merely symbols of sin? Surely Pearl is tedious and sometimes irritating if this is her sole symbolic function. Why does Chillingworth wither and die soon after Dimmesdale confesses? Why does Hawthorne at this point make Pearl the richest heiress in America?

The most damaging flaw in the conventional interpretation is that it fails almost completely to comprehend the language of the book. As one critic remarked years ago, Hawthorne's style is an "intense essence of the language, . . . his words conveying not only a meaning, but more than they appear to mean. They point onward or upward or downward."[5] One of the aims of this chapter will be to elucidate the book's unique language pattern. But before this can be accomplished, several preliminary steps must be taken. After a general statement of the book's subject, the allegorical significance of Pearl and Roger Chillingworth will be established. Once this is clear, the book's structure may be outlined. Only then can we proceed to a consideration of its guiding metaphor, the Tongue of Flame.

Like many great tragedies, *The Scarlet Letter* deals with the quest for truth, the revelation of secrets. First one riddle is solved, then another, until at the close the reader has been

---

[5] Quoted in George P. Lathrop, *A Study of Hawthorne* (Houghton Mifflin Company, Boston, 1876), p. 229.

drawn up to the ultimate revelation—the secret of man's moral growth. This will remain a mystery, however, because, like the Passion of Christ, it involves an eternal paradox: the mundane wisdom of man is insanity to God, and untempered celestial wisdom is equally insane in the social world. The mature insight of Oedipus coincides with his physical blindness and banishment; Arthur Dimmesdale purifies himself at the terrible human cost of sin, physical decay, and death. The crucial moment occurs when the emotionally involved reader or spectator raises and ennobles his own perspective so that he sees not only the agony but also the purification.

In *The Scarlet Letter* the quest for truth is an effort to know Pearl. As every reader of the book recognizes, she is the scarlet letter incarnate. But as the visible embodiment of truth about the particular sin, she becomes by extension the universal truth about the Original Sin. In a notebook entry, Hawthorne had written in 1841: "Is truth a fantasy which we are to pursue forever and never grasp?" Pearl, whose inscrutable black eyes invest her with a "strange remoteness and intangibility," is a dramatization of this passage. As truth's reflector, she rejects all half-truths, including those of the Puritans. Hawthorne adroitly manipulates the archaisms of the townspeople in order to indicate Pearl's symbolic function. When Chillingworth, for instance, asks a bystander about the identity of Pearl's father, the reply is: "*Of a truth,* friend, that matter remaineth a riddle" (V, 84).

Though Pearl's full significance will emerge only when we see her in relation to other characters, there is another aspect of her role that deserves mention here. She possesses "a native grace." In naming her, Hester has identified the child with the pearl of great price (Matt. 13: 45–46) the *pretiosa margarita.* This pearl has often been interpreted as Christ by the theologians, but it has also been construed as everlasting life or beatitude—the soul, either undefiled or redeemed in baptism. In "The Intelligence Office," Hawthorne had defined the pearl as "the soul of celestial purity" (II, 370). Pearl's name, her attire, and her very being thus sum up the riddle of human existence, in which man's insanity is heaven's sense. "Man had marked this woman's sin by a scarlet letter, which had such potent and disastrous efficacy that no human sympathy could reach her, save it were sinful like herself. God, as a direct consequence of the sin which man thus punished, had given her a lovely child, whose place was on that same dishonored bosom, to connect her parent for ever with the race and descent of mortals, and to be finally a blessed soul in heaven!" Pearl is a holy spirit, "worthy to have been brought forth in Eden; worthy to have been left there, to be the plaything of angels, after the world's first parents were driven out" (V, 114). But the temporal gap between the sin and the redemption must not be ignored; it is, in fact, at the heart of the story.

As an abstraction, Pearl is inflexible and inexorable. She has a "hard, metallic lustre" that needs grief to melt it and make her human. Both character and type, both natural and preternatural, she is in time and outside of it. She watches her reflection in the forest brook, the stream of time; a little later we are informed that "the soul beheld its features in the mirror of the passing moment" (V, 228). As a growing child, Pearl serves as an index to the passage of time in the narrative; as a symbol, she indicates to Hester and Arthur that truth cannot be perceived outside its temporal context.

These generalizations will derive further support when we see Pearl in relation to the two major characters. Meanwhile, having established as a working hypothesis at least that Pearl signifies truth and grace, we may turn to Roger Chillingworth. He has always been recognized as a personification, but it will not suffice to see him simply as evil incarnate. "Under the appellation of Roger Chillingworth . . . was hidden another name," and the name is not only Prynne—it is Guilt.[6] Hawthorne's portrayal of Chillingworth illustrates how beautifully his imagination could weld the abstract to the concrete. For the physician is interesting in his own right as an alchemist-psychiatrist manqué, who tries to solve the riddle of man's existence by logical or psychological analysis.

As a symbol of guilt, Chillingworth is a leech, draining his patient of nerve, will, and physical energy. But, as the whole book demonstrates, he is also the healer. Only by knowing him, confronting him face to face, is moral growth possible. Not that moral growth is guaranteed or that having this unwelcome guest is "fortunate"—it is simply inevitable in human existence. "The breach which guilt has once made into the human soul is never in this mortal state repaired. It may be watched and guarded; so that the enemy shall not force his way again *into the citadel,* and might even, in his subsequent assaults, select some other avenue, in preference to that where he had formerly succeeded. But there is still *the ruined wall*" (VI, 241). The italicized phrases remove all doubt of Chilingworth's identity. As guilt he invades the dwelling place, which, as we know, is customarily a symbol for the heart in Hawthorne's fiction. "My home," he tells Hester, "is where thou art and where he [the minister] is." Early in the book Chillingworth appears from nowhere to confront Hester in the prison cell of her heart; by the middle of the book he has insinuated himself into Dimmesdale's abode. "A deformed old figure, with a face that haunted men's memories longer than they liked," he gradually shrivels as

---

[6] This interpretation of Chillingworth's role was first suggested to me by Hillel Chodos and John L. Murphy.

The Tongue of Flame: The Scarlet Letter

Hester and Dimmesdale come closer to full recognition of him.

We are now perhaps in a position to understand why Hawthorne makes Pearl "the richest heiress in her day, in the New World." Allegorically, it is clear that the death of Chillingworth would automatically bequeath a massive legacy to Pearl. But the matter is not this simple. In the final pillory scene Pearl becomes humanized. As Dimmesdale ascends, she moves down from her allegorical function and into fully temporal existence. She shifts, as it were, from her role as the universal principle in the spiritual realm—an intuitive or natural language, a vital hieroglyphic—to a key role in the novel, the social world, whose basic medium is money.[7] Hawthorne returns her to the Old World with the riches from the New, giving her a solid social standing.

Once we identify Pearl and Chillingworth, the structural outline of *The Scarlet Letter* is clearly revealed. The first third of the book (Chapters I to VIII) concerns Hester's limited ascension. When she ascends the platform, she stands out in sharp contrast to the flint-faced, manlike women who surround her. Every inch a woman in her dual role as sinner and saint, Hester reaches the peak of her moral development

---

[7] The philosopher whose writings furnish one of the closest parallels to Hawthorne's thought is Johann Georg Hamann. Note, for instance, this passage:

"*Money* and *language* are two subjects whose investigation is as profound and abstract as their use is universal. Both stand in a closer relationship than one might presume. The theory of one explains the theory of the other; therefore they seem to flow from common sources. The wealth of all human knowledge rests on the exchange of words. . . . On the other hand, all the goods of civil or social life have reference to money as their universal standard." (Hamann's italics.) Quoted in James C. O'Flaherty, *Unity and Language: A Study in the Philosophy of Johann Georg Hamann* (University of North Carolina Press, Chapel Hill, N.C., 1952), p. 30.

in this section. She openly recognizes her guilt in Chapter III; she accepts the letter as Chillingworth's vital surrogate in Chapter IV; she grasps the truth intuitively through her art in Chapters V and VI; and she educates the leading members of the community in the meaning of that art in Chapters VII and VIII.

The middle third of the book (Chapters IX to XVI) is concerned with the burden of guilt and where it should reside. It is subdivided by the midnight pillory scene in the middle of the book. In Chapters IX to XII we see that guilt has been shifted almost completely from the woman to the man (Chillingworth now lives with Dimmesdale); and in the counterbalancing Chapters XIII to XVI we observe what has happened to the woman as a result of this shifting of responsibility.

The final third (Chapters XVII to XXIV) deals with Dimmesdale's ascension, which begins with the forest interview and ends with the revelation during the New England holiday. Where Hester's ascension was limited, his is complete; where she has been associated (though, as Hawthorne puts it, only "by contrast") with Divine Maternity, Dimmesdale attains the Word Incarnate. The book moves, therefore, from recognition through obscurity to revelation, from the light of Hester's ascension through the dark night of the soul to the final light of Dimmesdale's ascension. And the final symbol, as we shall see, sums up the whole action.

We may now pause to consider what is likely to be the major objection to this interpretation. If Chillingworth represents guilt, it may be asked, what happens to the sin of adultery upon which the whole book is based? The question is not only relevant but of the utmost importance for a grasp of the book's archetypal meaning. The reader may well be asked to see Chillingworth both as wronged husband and as guilt, but he is quite right in insisting that the sin ought to have meaning from both perspectives. The answer is that it does; it has a literal meaning in both senses of the word *literal:* "nonfigurative" and "original." All readers have noticed that the actual sin is prior to the action of the book. Of course it is prior; it is the literal, the Original Sin. Why did Hester marry Chillingworth? Why was Zenobia wedded to Westervelt? Why is Miriam linked to the "model"? Why did Eve allow herself to be seduced by Satan, thus fouling her perfect union with God? Why did all evil spring from Pandora's box? On this archetypal level, the timeless abstractions represented by Pearl and Chillingworth remain constant, but, like the man and the woman, they are stripped of their names and location. The "special reference to New England" is gone, and all that remains is the basic relation between man, woman, and Deity. *The Scarlet Letter* is seen not as romance but as myth—the story of man and woman in a fallen, that is, human, world. Like Rappaccini's garden, life in this "Eden of the present world" is an adulteration of God's original creation. The woman has broken her covenant with God in order to seek the kind of knowledge that is man's province; the man has broken his covenant with God in order to know the woman. As a result, life is such "commixture, and, as it were, *adultery*" that "the production" is "no longer of God's making" (II, 128).

Thus Hawthorne educates us once again in the given conditions of human life. Originally—that is, in his youth and before this book has begun—man's role, as we have seen, is speculation; it is a rootless gamble in space, the discovery of new particulars, the exploration of new fields, physical or intellectual. For maturity, however, man needs to leave this world of the first name and become involved through passion with the woman and her temporal burden. Originally, woman's role is investment; she brings to the man a dowry from the past. Without the man she lingers, literally or figuratively, in the Old World, in the ancestral homestead, buried under the patronymic. Without him she lives in time-drenched darkness; without her he is blanked out in the glare of space. Their union depends upon man's vulnerable area, his heart, and upon woman's, her head. After the union, which is where this book begins, the man wears his hand over his heart; the woman wears a cap over her head. After their union there is an exaggerated inversion of roles: the man, like Milton's Adam, is overwhelmed by a sense of time, of all history; the woman, like Milton's Eve, is blinded by speculation, offering noble but misguided ways of thwarting time. A reassertion of their natural roles, balanced and tempered by their new knowledge, must be effected if they are to find "the oneness of their being" in Pearl and re-establish something like their original relation to God.

Important though it is, we should not become fixed on the archetypal plane of interpretation. On this level all Hawthorne's romances are variants of essentially the same situation. They all involve a man (or his symbolic equivalent), a woman (or her substitute), their guilt, and their possible redemption. These are the given elements in the riddle of moral growth; they are the skeleton upon which all of Hawthorne's best work is based; but to fix our gaze unremittingly upon them is to lose the living letter of the romance. We join Melville's Bartleby and stare at the colorless wall of universals; we are stationary and not particular; we work in the Dead Letter Office.

Perhaps the best way of returning to the flesh and blood of the romance is to consider its guiding metaphor, the Tongue of Flame. Hawthorne derives this figure from the description in Acts 2:3–4 of the descent of the Holy Ghost upon the chosen disciples: "And there appeared unto them cloven tongues like as of fire, and it sat upon each of them. And they were all filled with the Holy Ghost. . . ." However, Hawthorne interprets this gift in his own way. The tongues of flame symbolize not the power of speech in all languages but the ability to address "the whole human brotherhood in the heart's native language" (V, 173). The Tongue of Flame is intuitive communication, the expression of "the highest truths through the humblest medium of familiar words and images."

I call this the crucial metaphor because ultimately the Tongue of Flame comes to be identical with the letter of scarlet, and its revelation consummates a process that goes on throughout the book. The quest for truth in *The Scarlet Letter* takes the specific and time-honored form of seeking to unite the Word and the Light in the Act. The Flame, or the Light, is vision—both insight and, as Sophia called it, "outsight"; it is the ability to see both the old universal patterns and the new particulars; and it is not only vision but revelation. The Word is the utterance and the investment; it comprises the tradition, the rhetorical and moral discipline, the communion, the surname; but it is also the new clothing, the new foliage, the new name. Both categories, therefore, contain the possibility of looking in opposite directions: backward and forward in time, inward and outward in space.

Thus *The Scarlet Letter,* like *Oedipus Tyrannus* and *King Lear,* is about ways of seeing. Many of the chapter titles— "The Interview," "The Interior of a Heart," "The Minister's Vigil," "Another View of Hester"—spring from the effort to gain a better perspective, a clearer view of the truth. Some of the book's key words retain vestiges of their original meaning in expressing this emphasis upon vision: "scene," "witness," "interview," "spectacle," "perspective," "speculation," "spectator," and "respectable." From the initial pillory scene, where Hester finds a "point of view," to the end, when she "glanced her sad eyes downward at the scarlet letter," the book deals with different kinds of vision.

But vision alone is insufficient as a means of conversion. To "be true," as the book's moral indicates, one must also "utter," make plain, "show freely" to others the secret of his identity. As the spirit is clothed in flesh and the flesh is clothed in garments, so ideas are clothed in words. The outer garments may be true to the inner reality: Hester's ascension is a mute utterance made manifest by the letter which society has vested upon her and which she has embroidered. Or they may be false covering: Dimmesdale's ascension at the close depends upon his willingness to divest himself of the priestly robe. Most of the garments in the book are accurate reflections of character. The massive women in the first pillory scene are swathed in petticoats and farthingales that match their "boldness and rotundity of speech"; Governor Bellingham's rigid devotion to outward forms may be seen in the hollow suit of armor, and his head and heart are separated by an imposing ruff; Mistress Hibbins wears a triple ruff for the same reason; the sea captain, the sailors, and the Indians express their individuality in their garb of scarlet and gold.

The Light is a process of seeing and disclosing; the Word is a process of uttering and investing; the Act is the intuitive union of both. Truth comes as a reward for intellectual discipline and human sympathy, but the ultimate incarnation that unites light and letter, spirit and flesh can only *be*. This intuition may be simply a sign, like Pearl's gestures, or a facial expression, like Chillingworth's when he discovers the letter on Dimmesdale's breast. More significant expression is achieved in art: Hester's needlework, Chillingworth's psychiatric alchemy, and Dimmesdale's Election Sermon. The highest form of intuitive truth, however, is the life that is patterned as a work of art. To make one's life a parable is to be the word incarnate; from one perspective, Dimmesdale's final symbolic gesture approaches this saintly level.

The action of the book shows how the two major characters are transformed when they join the Word and the Light in their actions and their art. Pearl, of course, does not change except at the end when she loses her allegorical function and becomes humanized. To know her in full context is the object of the quest; as a living hieroglyphic, a "character of flame," she unites language and vision in symbol. In so far as he is a character, Roger Chillingworth seeks to learn her origin and identity. He succeeds by inhumanely uniting his dim but penetrating gaze with amoral lore, both Indian and civilized, to perfect his art. But he is more significant in his allegorical relation to Hester and Arthur than he is as a character.

The main action concerns Hester Prynne and Arthur Dimmesdale as they seek transformation. Hester attains her most nearly complete vision in the first third of the book. She is seen: the object of "universal observation," she feels the "heavy weight of a thousand unrelenting eyes upon her" as she presents a living sermon to those who witness the spectacle. "Transfigured" by the scarlet letter, she discovers that the platform offers perspective in every direction. It enables her to look inward and backward to her parents, her former home, and her guilt; downward to the living realities of her present, the infant and the letter; and, for the only time in the book, upward, to the balcony where authority is seated.

The clarity of her vision at this point in the book is emphasized by the "recognition" scene. Though forced upon her by the community, it is an open recognition of guilt. Standing on her pedestal, Hester squarely faces the stranger who could not be buried in the sea or the wilderness and fixes her gaze upon him—"so fixed a gaze, that, at moments of intense absorption, all other objects in the visible world seemed to vanish, leaving only him and her. Such an interview, perhaps would have been more terrible than even to meet him as she now did, with the hot, mid-day sun burning down upon her face, and lighting up its shame" (V, 85). This lucid "interview" between Hester and Roger Chillingworth is interrupted by one of the preachers of the word, John Wilson, who urges her to "hearken," though he is poorly qualified to "step forth, as he now did, and meddle with a question of human guilt" (V, 87).

Nevertheless, Hester's ascension is limited. She sees the truth, but she will not utter the word. Heeding Chillingworth's gesture of secrecy, she does not publicly identify him. She has been educated under Dimmesdale's "preaching of the word"; she listens to his eloquent appeal for her to reveal her fellow-sinner's identity—an appeal that prompts a half-pleased, half-plaintive murmur from Pearl; but Hester will not utter the name. "She will not speak." And when her actual interview with Roger Chillingworth occurs, not in the mid-day sun but in the dark prison, we have the first clue to what will eventually develop into merely superficial penance. In this "dismal apartment" of her heart, she is confronted by her guilt, who lays his long forefinger on the scarlet letter and makes it his symbolic representative. Chillingworth then enjoins her to keep his identity secret, especially from Dimmesdale. "Recognize me not, by word, by sign, by look!" She determines to recognize only the letter and not the living embodiment of her guilt; and her release from confinement immediately follows.

Hester has thus gained only a partial insight from her plunge into the pit and her consequent ascent. She decides to stay in Boston, reasoning that the scene of her sin should become the scene of her penance. Since her deepest motive, however, is to remain close to her lover, her ideas about expiating the sin are partly rationalization. Nevertheless, she does resist a retreat into space—eastward to Europe or westward into the wilderness. Uniting the perspective gained from the pillory with the word, the letter branded upon her, she puts off the old garments and finds a new self in her art.

Only in her art does Hester begin to find grace and to grasp the truth; that is, only in her art does she come to know Pearl. Her needlework is an "act of penance," a product of delicate imaginative skill, and under other circumstances it might have been the "passion of her life." Through it she becomes involved with birth and death, with the social hierarchy, with all phases of community life (save marriage), adding the hidden sins and wounds of mankind to her own burden. Allowing her imagination full play, she has wrought better than she knew in creating Pearl's attire, and she has been imaginatively right in naming the child.

Unsatisfied with the intuitive vision of her art, however, Hester is tortured by her inability to understand Pearl in any rational medium. Her offspring is fanciful, spritelike, inscrutable; in her wild, bright, deep-black eyes she reflects the truth; but reflection can also foster diabolical illusion. "Brooding over all these matters, the mother felt like one who has evoked a spirit, but, by some irregularity in the process of conjuration, has *failed to win the master-word* that should control this new and incomprehensible intelligence" (V, 117–18). At the end of Chapter VII she makes an abortive effort to grasp the truth intellectually, putting the child through a half-earnest, half-playful catechism. "Art thou my child, in very truth?" she asks. "Tell me, then, what thou art, and who sent thee hither." (We notice, again, how Hawthorne suggests Pearl's fusion of art and truth in the archaisms of the dialogue.) But Pearl is not to be apprehended in this manner, and she further punishes Hester by refusing to admit a heavenly Father so long as the earthly father is concealed.

The superiority of Hester's artistic insight over the hollow rigidity of the orthodox is made clear when she and Pearl educate the highest members of the local hierarchy in the Governor's hall. She goes there to deliver a pair of embroidered gloves—we later learn that "a pure hand needs no glove to cover it" (V, 192)—and to argue for her right to keep Pearl. Bellingham's personality is neatly expressed in his stuccoed house, his gilded volumes, and the suit of armor. His views toward Hester and Pearl reveal themselves in the grotesque, inhuman distortions reflected by the armor. Cut off like Prufrock from spontaneity and fruitful emotion, he appears in an elaborate ruff that causes his head "to look not a little like that of John the Baptist in a charger." His astonishment at seeing the truth incarnate in his house is quite understandable. "I have never seen the like," he says, in unwitting self-criticism. "How gat such a guest into my hall?"

It soon becomes clear that the "truths of heaven and earth" cannot be seen through the catechism. Pearl, though unacquainted with the "outward form" of the *New England Primer* or the Westminster Catechism, could have undergone a fair examination in these works. But she naturally evades the question of the clergyman John Wilson about her origin, finally informing him that she had been plucked from the wild rose bush. The stunned Governor asserts that she is "in the dark," thereby provoking Hester into a heated illumination of his own blindness. "*See ye not*, she is the scarlet letter, only capable of being loved, and so endowed with a millionfold the power of retribution for my sin?" Turning to Dimmesdale, she cries: "*Speak for me* . . . thou knowest what is in my heart, and what are a mother's rights, and how much the stronger they are, when that mother has but her child and the scarlet letter! *Look thou to it!*" "There is truth in what she says," answers the minister, who has always been more responsive to the word than to the vision. Upon the Governor's request that he "make that plain," Dimmesdale teaches him what is expressed by Hester's art—namely that Pearl is both burden and blessing.

During the first third of the book, therefore, Hester, her glowing letter, and Pearl are as lights shining in the darkness of the community. The minister, meanwhile, fasts and vigils in the darkness and preaches words that place him in a false light. He attains a new perspective, however, when he begins to live with his guilt. When Chillingworth moves in with him, Dimmesdale finds in the physician's mind a remarkable depth and scope. "It was as if a window were thrown open," but "the air was too fresh and chill to be long breathed with comfort." Later, as Chillingworth keeps probing for "God's own truth," both men hear Pearl's laughter outside. "Looking instinctively from the open window," the minister sees Hester and Pearl in the adjacent burial ground. Here, seen from the new perspective and clearly outlined in the bright sunlight of the summer day, is the very truth that Chillingworth is seeking, but neither man can perceive it. Chillingworth looks at Pearl and asks, "What, in Heaven's name, is she?" And Dimmesdale is unable to explain her "principle of being."

The comprehension and communication of religious truth demands an intuitive fusion of language and vision. Hawthorne suggests that if Dimmesdale had not sinned, his native gifts would have placed him among the group of true saintly fathers whose only fault was their failure to communicate the highest truths to the populace. "All that they lacked was the gift that descended upon the chosen disciples at Pentecost, in tongues of flames; symbolizing, it would seem, not the power of speech in foreign and unknown languages, but that of addressing the whole human brotherhood in the heart's native language. These fathers, otherwise so apostolic, lacked Heaven's last and rarest attestation of their office, The Tongue of Flame. They would have vainly sought—had they ever dreamed of seeking—to express the highest truths through the humblest medium of familiar words and images" (V, 173). But Dimmesdale's burden keeps him on a level with the lowest. His congregation worships him; their adoration intensifies his guilty anguish; and his suffering heightens his fervor. Yet before he can truly speak with the Tongue of Flame, he must not only relate but reveal. He has already *spoken* the truth—confessed his sin—but in such abstract terms that he well knew "*the light* in which his vague confession would be viewed" (V, 176).

So long as they are covert, the minister's gestures are but a mockery of penitence, and his cloistral flagellations, fasts, and vigils are unavailing. The magnificent midnight scaffold scene dramatizes the various degrees of moral blindness in the community and throws the falsity of the minister's rationalizations into sharp relief. Clothed as if he were going to attend public worship, he ascends the platform, which is cloaked in darkness. Much more perceptive than the Governor, who can "see but little further than a mill-stone" in the darkness, he also has a more exalted perspective than John Wilson's. That elderly clergyman approaches the platform, but his glimmering lantern reveals only "the muddy pathway" beneath his feet.

Dimmesdale still persists in his argument, eternally true perhaps, but humanly false, that revelation must wait until

judgment day. Hester and Pearl have joined him on the platform; he has been infused with new life as he takes Pearl's
hand; but the tableau that follows is a visualization of his
argument. For the awesome light of the meteor provides a
kind of noon, "as if it were the light that is to reveal all
secrets." It is like the day of doom, and in this lurid light the
minister sees the ambiguity of his argument without being
consciously aware of it. Though he gazes toward the zenith
he is at the same time perfectly aware that Pearl is pointing
toward Roger Chillingworth, his earthly guilt. He is close to
perceiving the relation between the woman, their mutual
guilt and their possible salvation; but when he asks Pearl to
translate this vision into rational terms, he is unable to understand her natural or intuitive language. She speaks "in a
tongue unknown to the erudite clergyman." Nevertheless,
his revelation has unconsciously begun. He has divested himself of part of his hollow armor—the black glove.

The middle third of the book is perfectly and ironically
balanced, for as the minister is struggling toward outsight
and disclosure, Hester is seeking insight and utterance. Her
moral predicament during the past few years has been just
the reverse of his. Outwardly she has been a penitent sinner,
and by her good works she has transmuted the letter into a
badge of mercy. To many, the letter has "the effect of a
cross on a nun's bosom." But her nominal penance is just as
incomplete as Dimmesdale's closeted flagellations. Since the
"interview" of Chapter IV she has not acknowledged her
connection with Roger Chillingworth, and his symbol, the
letter, has ceased being a vital one for her. Without the
spirit, the letter killeth: the *A* may now stand for "Able," but
there is "nothing in Hester's bosom, to make it ever again the
pillow of Affection," unless another transfiguration occurs.
She has become a mannish vagrant, speculating in the

gloomy labyrinth of the mind. It is a kind of dissipation in which her natural role as woman has evaporated into space. The Word, outwardly imposed and outwardly worn, has failed in its traditional rhetorical discipline. "The scarlet letter had not done its office."

Thus the midnight scaffold scene has been a dark night of the soul for her as well as for the minister. But as a result of Dimmesdale's changed aspect, she has been given a "new theme for reflection." She resolves to confront her guilt and confess it to the minister. "I would speak a word with you," she says to Chillingworth, "a word that concerns us much." The word amounts to a new acceptance of her responsibility in the sin; and her emotions as she watches Chillingworth depart throw "a dark light" on her state of mind, "revealing much that she might not otherwise have acknowledged to herself." Pearl seems much closer and more earnest than ever before. But Hester is not yet ready for the utterance of the whole truth. To Pearl's relentless questions, Hester can only reply, "Hold thy tongue," and threaten to shut the child in *her* dark closet.

The complex interweaving of utterance and vision, invest-ment and speculation, time and space reaches a peak in the forest interview. Dimmesdale tells Hester of his torture, which has been augmented by his native gifts: "Canst thou deem it, Hester, a consolation, that I must stand up in my pulpit, and meet so many eyes turned upward to my face, as if the *light of heaven* were beaming from it!—must see my flock hungry for the truth, and listening to my words *as if a tongue of Pentecost were speaking!* and then look inward, and discern the black reality of what they idolize?" Hester gently suggests that the sin has been left behind, that peni-tence is sealed and witnessed by good works. But the pastor knows better. Then she conquers her fears and utters her responsibility for the guilt that now resides with him. "Dost thou not *see* what I would *say?* That old man!—the physician!—he whom they call Roger Chillingworth! he was my husband." Like Milton's Adam, Arthur sternly repels her; and then his heart relents.

At this point Hester offers a way of lightening the burden in their share of woe. Never—not even in the exhortations of Emerson and Thoreau—has the vision of dawn, the promise of America, the dream of a second chance found more deeply felt utterance than in her appeal, as she urges the time-drenched man to recover himself, to put on a new name and leave the ruin behind him. "Preach! Write! Act! Do anything save to lie down and die!" The closing formula of her brief but eloquent sermon is "Up and away!" The fact that this phrase is likely to call up for some modern readers a vision of the gaudily vested Superman may seem unfortunate. But this association is not entirely irrelevant: as we know, one consequence of the doctrine of self-reliance, was its distortion into a grossly materialized version of the superman. And the modern connotations of the phrase, voiced as it is by the woman, simply point up the inversion of roles that climaxes the forest scene. She has grown eloquent while he is now silent; she has lost insight while he is gaining outsight. The parishioner is now preaching to the pastor. Dimmesdale, on the other hand, in whose eyes "a fitful light" has been kindled by Hester's enthusiasm, now gazes upon her with a "look in which hope and joy shone out." She has spoken "what he vaguely hinted at but dared not speak."

As the succeeding events reveal, Hester has preached a half-truth. She has rightly told him to be a man, to exert his protestant function of penetrating into space and conquering new fields. All this he could do—alone. What Hester does not see is that if she is to go with him, he must accept the catholic involvement in guilt-stained time that is the essence of her womanhood. She has usurped the masculine prerogative of speculation, and her intellectual wanderings have been so undisciplined that they have become obscure. In the gloom of the wilderness or the blankness of space, nothing of temporal or moral significance can be seen.

That her proposal is only half valid may be discerned from her symbolic relation to Pearl and the stream of time. Hester would like to retain only the pleasant aspects of the past. She throws off the scarlet letter (it lands, however, on the "hither verge" of the stream of time); she removes the formal cap that confines her hair, resuming "her sex, her youth, and the whole richness of her beauty" from "what men call the irrevocable past." And she tells Arthur: "Thou must know Pearl. . . . Thou hast seen her,—yes, I know it!—but thou wilt see her now with other eyes. She is a strange child. I hardly comprehend her." With his newly discovered vision, the minister can see Pearl, standing a good way off on the other side of the brook. But neither he nor Hester is yet skilled to read "the character of flame," the "oneness of their being." Pearl will not join them, for wholeness is not achieved by drawing a sharp boundary between the worlds of past and present. Her symbolic gestures, reflected in the stream, indicate that their proposed escape from time into motion and space is an unrealizable dream—or at least can be effected only at the cost of leaving their salvation behind.

√Though Hester desperately clings to the hope of drowning her guilt in the deep sea, she now recognizes that the forest cannot hide it. The moment of inspiration has passed. By flinging the letter "into infinite space" she had drawn "an hour's free breath," but now the burden must be resumed. The child rejoins her mother, but between Pearl and the minister there is no expression, no communion. He awkwardly impresses a kiss on her brow, which she hastily washes off in the brook.

The precise nature of the minister's transformation in the forest is once again worked out in terms of the Word and the Light. He has stripped away the old words; he has discarded his old self amid the decaying leaves "like a cast-off garment." The scales have dropped from his eyes; he has attained an Emersonian vision. But his old insight has been temporarily obliterated. His condition is indicated by Hawthorne's complex moral topography. The pathway in the woods seems "wilder, more uncouth with its rude natural obstacles, and less trodden by the foot of man, than he remembered it on his outward journey." On the one hand, he is closer to the freedom of individual growth, less hampered by the principles and prejudices of the social system; on the other, he is, as the chapter title indicates, "the minister in a maze"—more deeply involved in a moral wilderness with its "plashy places" and its "clinging underbrush."

In this mood, it is all that Dimmesdale can do to keep from mocking his old words. Intoxicated and unbalanced by the heady wine of the new, he runs into a series of delightfully wrought encounters that anticipate Clifford Pyncheon's escape from his past in *The House of the Seven Gables.* He has temporarily substituted the undisciplined "vision" for communion; thus when he meets a hoary old deacon he has to forcibly restrain himself from "uttering certain blasphemous suggestions that entered his mind, respecting the communion supper. He absolutely trembled and turned pale as ashes, lest his tongue should wag itself, in utterance of these horrible matters." He resists the temptation to blight the innocence of a virgin with "but one wicked look" and the development of evil with "but a word." All his other misadventures stem from his rejection of the old rhetorical discipline. The sinister side of his revolt is cleverly shown by the pompous modern jargon of his conversation with Mistress Hibbins, the embodiment of ubiquitous evil. "I profess, madam," he says, with "a grave obeisance, such as the lady's rank" demands, "I profess, on my conscience and character, that I am utterly bewildered as touching the purport of your words! I went not into the forest to seek a potentate; neither do I, at any future time, design a visit thither, with a view to gaining the favor of such a personage."

After the vision of the forest interview, what Dimmesdale clearly needs now is to be nourished by a communion with the tomb-fed faith and the tome-fed wisdom of the past. In order to grasp the truth in his art form, he must return to the rich intellectual resources of the study, adjacent to the graveyard. "Here he had studied and written; here, gone through fast and vigil, and come forth half alive; here, striven to pray; here, borne a hundred thousand agonies! There was the Bible, in its rich old Hebrew, with Moses and the Prophets speaking to him, and God's voice through all!" White and speechless, he has been able to confront Roger Chillingworth squarely; he has withstood the travail of temptation in the wilderness; and now he is able to join the new vision with the rich utterances of the past. The long fast is over. Partaking of supper, he composes, as if divinely inspired, the flaming rhetoric of the Election Sermon. This is *his* new field; this is his true dawn; and as the golden sunrise beams in his study, he is seen with the pen still between his fingers and "a vast, immeasurable tract of written space behind him."

The Election Sermon itself cannot be rationally reproduced—it is heard and felt. To Hester, who is outside the church, it sounds like the great organ music of "a tongue

native to the human heart, wherever educated." In its under-
tone may be detected the deep ache at the heart of human
life itself—a sense of atonement not only for the individual
sin but for Original Sin. The crowd inside the church is spell-
bound at the close of the sermon, profoundly silent as if they
had heard "the utterance of oracles." Then they gush forth
from the doors, feeling the need of "other breath, more fit to
support the gross and earthly life into which they relapsed,
than that atmosphere which the preacher had converted into
words of flame." The subject of the sermon, as it is later revealed, is akin to the theme of the book: "the relation between the Deity and the communities of mankind, with a
special reference to the New England which they were planting here in the wilderness." The minister prophesies a high
and glorious destiny for these communities, just as God has
providentially transformed his own moral wilderness into
glory.

The last ascension scene captures with terse, compelling
inevitability the paradox that lies at the heart of tragedy and
Christianity. Time and eternity intersect on the platform of
the pillory as Dimmesdale, "in the name of Him, so terrible
and so merciful, who gives me grace at this last moment,"
makes the final revelation and is at last united with Pearl.
With his vision into eternity, he asks Hester, "Is not this
better . . . than what we dreamed of in the forest?" Her answer is the temporal one: "I know not. . . . Better? Yea; so
we may both die, and little Pearl die with us." Even her last
hope—for a specific reunion in an afterlife—is clothed in
earthly terms, and in his dying breath Dimmesdale offers her
no encouragement.

The various reactions of the crowd to Dimmesdale's revelation are presented in ascending order from the crude to
the spiritual. The first two conjectures about the origin of

HAWTHORNE'S TRAGIC VISION

the letter on his breast—that it was self-imposed torture, or that Roger Chillingworth wrought it with his poisonous drugs—are the most naturalistic and the least valid. A third group—"those best able to appreciate the minister's peculiar sensibility and the wonderful operation of his spirit upon the body"—see the letter as a psychic cancer that gradually manifested itself physically. But the last group is the most interesting. These "highly respectable witnesses" are "spectators of the whole scene," and they see the minister as a saint. They associate his final action with Christ's sympathy for the adulteress, and they think Dimmesdale so shaped the manner of his death as to make of it a parable, illustrating "that in the view of Infinite Purity, we are sinners all alike."

Having stated this view in more detail than any of the others, Hawthorne then explicitly questions it in the light of common sense. A clue to the ambiguity here is offered by the meanings of the word *respectable*. In its usual sense, the adjective tells us that these witnesses were among the more pious and pompous members of the community, stubbornly refusing to see any evil in the high representatives of their society. Yet in a book where the language itself points back to the original—a book dealing with vision and language, where words like "spectator" and "speculation" are extremely significant—we begin to wonder about our easy rejection of these "respectable" witnesses. Etymologically, these are the spectators who *look back;* and from this point of view their version of the minister's life is the most original, the most spiritual of all.

Considerable evidence supporting their view may be found in Hawthorne's description of the New England holiday. Despite its sable tinge, there is an aura of hope. "For today," as Hester tells Pearl, "a new man is beginning to rule over them; and so—as has been the custom of mankind ever

since a nation was first gathered—they make merry and re-
joice; as if a good and golden year were at length to *pass
over* the poor old world." The new man is really Arthur
Dimmesdale. Having achieved individuation in the forest, ~~forest~~
he now returns to join the procession only to rise above it.
"The spiritual element took up the feeble frame, and carried
it along, unconscious of the burden and converting it to spirit
like itself."

But the whole truth is not distilled in the refined perception of the respectable witnesses. Their view must be considered along with the crude ideas of the materialists; and
the composite of the two is represented by those firmly
grounded in the temporal life who nevertheless appreciate
the minister's sensibility, the interaction of flesh and spirit.
The "moral," which at first sight seems to be an oversimplifi-
cation, should be read in this light. To "be true," one must not
mean but be. The truth, that is to say, can only be grasped
in its total living context; and since this comprehensive view
is impossible from any single human perspective, the closest
we can come to it is through "expression"—art, symbol, gesture, or parable—a showing "of some trait" from which the
totality may be inferred.

At the end we are left with the symbol into which the
whole meaning of the book has been distilled. Around the
letter have gathered not only the explicit associations of
Adultress, Able, Affection, and Angel but also the myriad
subtle suggestions of art, atonement, ascension, and the Acts
of the Apostles. Here is the *A,* each limb of which suggests
an ascension, with Pearl the link between the two; here is the
sable background of the Puritan community; and fused in
the entire symbol are the flesh and the spirit, the word and
the light, the letter *A,* gules. Hawthorne seized upon the
heraldic wording partly because of its rich poetic associa-

tions but also because "gules" is the perfect word with which to conclude the book. It means "scarlet," of course, but it originates from the Latin *gula,* meaning "throat." Here condensed in one word is the Tongue of Flame; here, joining the language patterns of vision and eloquence, is the perfect capstone for Hawthorne's symbolic structure.

vii ─

Evolution and Regeneration:
The House of the Seven Gables

IN *The House of the Seven Gables* the basic elements of the moral situation are once again placed before us. But the characters, tone, and guiding metaphor have radically changed from those of *The Scarlet Letter*. The ambiguous qualities of womanhood are subsumed in the dark house; the masculine traits are symbolized in the various inhabitants of the street; and the central metaphor is drawn from the process of evolution. Before we proceed to the book itself we ought to consider briefly Hawthorne's attitude toward evolution.

Nothing could be further from Darwinian descendental-

HAWTHORNE'S TRAGIC VISION

ism than the brief report on "Species of Men" that Hawthorne cranked out for *The American Magazine of Useful
and Entertaining Knowledge* in August, 1836. Using the
classifications of Linnaeus for his guide, he compared men
with orangutans and concluded in favor of Homo sapiens.[1]
In later years, when he visited the British Museum, the Eth-
nographical Rooms left him cold. "I care little for the varieties of the human race," he said, "all that is really important
and interesting being found in our own variety" (*English
Notebooks*, 611). Indeed, one interested in the relation of
science to American literature might draw up a list of items
showing Hawthorne's apathy toward the contemporary furor
about evolution: no references to Lamarck or Lyell; no reaction to Chambers' *Vestiges of the Natural History of Creation* (1844); no evidence that he knew of Charles Darwin's
existence; a lifelong indifference to fossils; little or no curiosity about geology and astronomy. Here surely is exemplified what Austin Warren meant when he said that Hawthorne was "nearly impervious to the intellectual movements
of his day."[2] All we have to do is contrast his notebooks with
Emerson's journals, studded with allusions to Lyell, Oken,
Goethe, Stallo, and Darwin.

Yet this is superficial and negative evidence. Though
Emerson was more interested in contemporary science, nothing he ever wrote compares with Hawthorne's artistic representation of growth, continuity, and change. Unimpressed by
collections of scientific data, Hawthorne was fascinated by
the interaction of past and present, heredity and environment. He was always a sympathetic and attentive observer
of plant life. What stimulated him was the process of growth:

[1] *Hawthorne as Editor*, ed. Arlin Turner (Louisiana State University
Press, Baton Rouge, La., 1941), pp. 209–10.
[2] Austin Warren, ed., *Hawthorne: Representative Selections* (American Book Company, New York, 1934), p. xi.

Evolution and Regeneration: The House of the Seven Gables

the development of the "crook-necked winter squashes, from the first little bulb with the withered blossom adhering to it, until they lay strewn upon the soil, big round fellows, hiding their heads beneath the leaves, but turning up their great yellow rotundities to the noontide sun" (II, 24). Gazing at his garden at "The Old Manse," he felt that "something worth living for had been done. A new substance was born into the world."

As he observed the cycle of the seasons and the maturing of his plants in the garden near the Concord River, Hawthorne naturally followed the practice of his time in drawing parallels between man and nature. But he never fell into the excesses of the German *Naturphilosophie,* blurring the distinctions between man and other forms of life. "However close upon our heels the inferiour tribes of creation may seem to tread," he wrote, "there is one great and invariable mark of distinction." Man has increasing knowledge and responsibility; the orangutan does not. The essential soundness of this position need not be labored today, since the spokesmen for a gladiatorial theory of existence have fallen into disrepute. But it is heartening to see the morality of knowledge and responsibility expounded by a modern authority on evolution. In *The Meaning of Evolution,* probably the best general explanation that has yet appeared, George Gaylord Simpson approaches his subject from a broad knowledge of paleontology, and thus his method is a far cry from Hawthorne's. In the second part of his book, however, Simpson searches for an evolutionary ethic. Distinguishing between the "old evolution" universal to all organisms and the "new evolution" peculiar to man, Simpson decries the fallacious tooth-and-claw morality of the early Darwinians. "The old evolution was and is essentially amoral. The new evolution involves knowledge, including the knowledge of good and evil."[3] Here he and Hawthorne are on common ground. This is the province of *The House of the Seven Gables*.

When it was first erected, the House of the Seven Gables typified the mechanical Colonel Pyncheon. But it has developed through the years until by Hepzibah's time it has become humanized. Hawthorne typically portrays this mellowing by making the house become almost organic. The Pyncheon elm "sweeps the whole black roof with its pendent foliage," so that the house seems "part of nature." In the yard and "especially in the angles of the building" can be seen "an enormous fertility of burdocks" with leaves two or three feet long. Green moss has gathered over the window and on the roof; flower shrubs (Alice's posies) appear in the nook between two of the gables (III, 43–44). The history of the house is thus a record of continuity and change and suggests the book's main problem, which, using the term in the mid-nineteenth-century sense, we may define as one of evolution. The explicitly stated theme is that "the weaknesses and defects, the bad passions, the mean tendencies, and the moral diseases which lead to crime are handed down from one generation to another, by a far surer process of transmission than human law" (III, 147). In short, Hawthorne is here concerned with the moral aspects of what in modern terms would be called the "ontogenetic problem," with the quite apparent but nonetheless mysterious similarities and differences that exist between progenitor and offspring. Like all his contemporaries, including Charles Darwin, he shared the assumption, stated most emphatically by Lamarck, that some acquired characteristics are inherited. Writing in the pre-Mendelian era, he also assumed that heredity factors are somehow transmitted "in the blood."

[3] George G. Simpson, *The Meaning of Evolution* (Yale University Press, New Haven, Conn., 1949), p. 311.

The fact that *The House of the Seven Gables* would now hardly bear scrutiny as a scientific treatise in genetics should not blind us to its essentially genetic point of view, in which an understanding of the house and its occupants depends upon knowledge of their history. The most obvious clues to the subject of the book are the terms used to describe the Pyncheons and the Maules. The old Colonel is called "the progenitor"; his offspring are "specimens of the breed"; the "elder stock" in this country have had "little or no intercourse" with the "English branch" of the family; Phoebe is "one little offshoot" who has acquired variety and hence new vitality. Her practical sense comes from her mother's side, while something about her mouth reminds Jaffrey of her father. Decrepit Hepzibah and recessive Clifford are paralleled by "a few species of antique and hereditary flowers, in no very flourishing condition" and more notably, of course, by the chickens—"pure specimens of a breed which had been transmitted down as an heirloom in the Pyncheon family." Like Hepzibah, the chickens have degenerated because they have been kept too pure a species. "These feathered people had existed too long in their distinct variety; a fact of which the present representatives, judging by their lugubrious deportment, seemed to be aware." Then there is the Pyncheon elm, the family tree, one branch of which represents Jaffrey Pyncheon and is transmuted to gold after his death (III, 77, 337). The Maules, on their side, have transmitted a "hereditary character of reserve" that has contributed to their poverty and isolation.

Evolution, as we know, favors those who have the most offspring, and Hawthorne did not ignore the sexual element in the genetic history of the Pyncheons. One of the ironies of this history has been the way in which the sexual aggressiveness of the dominant strain has limited its children. Colonel

HAWTHORNE'S TRAGIC VISION

Pyncheon "had worn out three wives" by the "remorseless weight and hardness of his character in the conjugal relation." The equally animalistic Jaffrey exhausts his wife in three or four years, and his only son dies of cholera. Hawthorne deftly hints at the Judge's sexual behavior by describing his contribution to agriculture "through the agency of the famous Pyncheon bull." The sterility of the recessive strain, on the other hand, can be seen in Clifford, who has "never quaffed the cup of passionate love," and Hepzibah, the "time-stricken virgin" who has never known "what love technically means." Thus, as Hawthorne rather laboriously puts it, "in respect to natural increase, the breed had not thriven."

The plot of the book and the moral growth of its characters depend upon a subtle interaction between heredity and environment, the house and the street. These two elements, introduced in the first paragraph and gradually developed into a "mighty contrast" (III, 68), need to be carefully examined, for they provide our clearest insight into the way in which Hawthorne fused biological, social, and moral materials into a work of art. The house is a complex symbol of various hereditary forces. On the whole it is, as Simpson has described heredity, "a conservative factor tending to keep succeeding generations within a common pattern."[4] Resembling a great human heart, which Hawthorne elsewhere described as "the great conservative," the house also objectifies the inner life of the psyche. Through its dusky mirror flow shades of the past that blend into the present (III, 330-32). Its realm is that of "real time," or duration, as Bergson described it;[5] within its shadowy depths the spatial elements of

4 *Ibid.*, p. 212.
5 Henri Bergson, *Creative Evolution*, trans. Arthur Mitchell (Henry Holt and Company, Inc., New York, 1911), pp. 37-40.

extension and solidity tend to melt away. This process is exemplified in the portrait of Colonel Pyncheon: its "physical outline and substance" seem to be "darkening away" as "the superficial coloring has been rubbed off by time" (III, 79).

As a veritable "womb of time," the house is also the repository of the word. Hidden within its depths are the "letters and parchments" that old Colonel Pyncheon had bequeathed to his posterity—documents that will turn out to be worthless for the present generation. Equally lifeless for Clifford and Hepzibah are volumes of what had once been brilliant comedies during the Restoration and in the eighteenth century. Hawthorne mentions Dryden's *Miscellany Poems, The Tatler,* and especially Pope's *The Rape of the Lock,* which was singled out, perhaps, because its title fits into the sexual imagery and the eventual penetration by Judge Pyncheon into the house. As Hepzibah reads aloud from these volumes, her croaking voice transforms their once witty pages into lugubrious monotony.

The orientation of the house signifies its place midway between two civilizations. It faces the commerce of the street on the west, while to the rear on the east is an old garden. Its exterior darkened by the "prevalent east wind," the house contains within its gloomy halls a map of what is consistently referred to as the "Eastern claim." Though the land itself is only as far east as Waldo County in Maine, it is associated with the "princely territory" of Europe and symbolizes the aristocratic tradition of the Pyncheon clan, with its "antique portraits, pedigrees, coats of arms." This trait was personified in "foreign-bred" Gervayse Pyncheon, grandson of the old Colonel, whose efforts to obtain the Eastern claim were motivated by his desire to return to England, "that more congenial home." His daughter Alice was also inordinately proud, but her beauty, her flowers, and her music indicate the beneficial contribution of the exotic strain. During her stay, the house seemed jolly-looking and alive, heated by the hearty warmth of the great chimney.

The darkness of the house, however, is more impressive than its vitality. Within its depths are shadowy emblems of the past, each representing evil geniuses (we would call them "genes") of the Pyncheon family. The ancestral chair is a reminder not only of the old Colonel but also of the family's susceptibility to apoplexy (Maule's curse); the portrait and the map are dimly visible tokens of his inflexible sternness and greed. The harpsichord is now like a coffin and recalls Alice Pyncheon's fatal pride. None of these objects can be distinguished very clearly in the darkness, but it is one of the book's purposes to show that they have an inescapable reality.

Certainly their burden weighs heavily upon the present incumbents of the house. Hepzibah's unbending and decadent gentility is matched by the stiff chairs, her beetle-browed frown by the front of the house as it lowers on the street. The essential nobility of her character is masked by her grotesque exterior. The exotic strain recurs in Clifford, whose undisciplined sensibility and faded beauty remind us of Gervayse Pyncheon and his daughter. The long intervening years and Clifford's unjust imprisonment have weakened and coarsened the traits of his ancestors. Where Gervayse had savored fine imported wines, Clifford voraciously gulps coffee and breakfast cakes (Hepzibah is unable to produce a meal from the cookbook full of English recipes); where Alice played hauntingly beautiful melodies on the harpsichord, Clifford must be content with their modern counterpart, the creaky music of the Italian's hurdy-gurdy.

To move from the sepulchral darkness of the house to the

Evolution and Regeneration: The House of the Seven Gables

dusty sunlight of the street is to discover the hubbub of the contemporary environment. Though Hawthorne occasionally describes the street as a quiet byway, he obviously intended to capture in it the whole throbbing turmoil of nineteenth-century life in this country. It is a struggle for existence, a "battle with one kind of necessity or another," in which the poorhouse awaits those who lose. The street becomes "a mighty river of life, massive in its tide," brimming with loquacious housewives and raucous vendors; the world is like a train or "an omnibus, with its populous interior, dropping here and there a passenger, and picking up another." In these two dominant images, Hawthorne clearly perceived that aspect of American society which Theodore Dreiser and H. L. Mencken were later to seize upon as characteristic: its bewildering and ceaseless fluidity. In its aimless flux some people rise above the surface while others submerge, and, as in Dreiser's *Sister Carrie,* there seems little real connection between individuals as they meet on the way up or down. The current of life on the train that carries Clifford and Hepzibah away from the old house is typical. "New people continually entered. Old acquaintances—for such they soon grew to be, in this rapid current of affairs—continually departed."

In a fluctuating society where the shadowy barriers of caste seem to have disappeared, external appearances and mechanical precision are of the utmost importance. It is a world of shimmering shop windows, a glittering bazaar dominated by "a multitude of perfumed and glossy salesmen, smirking, smiling, bowing, and measuring out the goods" (III, 67–68). Typified by the pantomime of the hurdy-gurdy operator, it is "an automatic community" in which the cobbler, the blacksmith, and the scholar dance to one identical tune, work with feverish activity, and "bring nothing finally

to pass." For in this epitome of life in the street, the movement of time, like the melody, is frozen in space. "At the ces-
sation of the music, everybody was petrified, at once, from
the most extravagant life into a dead torpor." The meanest
aspect of this life can be seen in the organ-grinder's monkey,
whose outstretched paw and "strangely man-like expression"
form an image of covetousness. "Doubtless, more than one
New-Englander passed by, and threw a look at the monkey,
and went on, without imagining how nearly his own moral
condition was here exemplified."

Where the house is organic, temporal, feminine, and integrated, the street is essentially mechanical, spatial, masculine, and atomistic—a congeries of inert particles related only
in so far as they are governed by the solar system. Judge
Pyncheon, Uncle Venner, and Holgrave are the street's chief
representatives. Its worst features, its incessant emphasis
upon the "big, heavy, solid unrealities" of gold, real estate,
and clothes, are embodied in the Judge. Distinguished by the
"studied propriety of his dress and equipment," he and his
benign smile are as superficial as the shine on his boots. In
ironic contrast to Hepzibah, the "snowy whiteness" of his
linen hides the dark, corpselike soul within. Like Mammon,
he is a creature of the pavement, keeping in constant touch
with it by means of his gold-headed cane. He is a super-
patriot: "The fate of the country is staked on the November
election" in which he hopes to become governor. A devotee
of the "scale and balance system," he wishes to retain of
time only what can be spread out all at once in space.[6]

The philosopher of the street is harmless Uncle Venner,
who has "studied the world at street corners." " 'Give no

[6] Compare Bergson's description in *ibid.*, p. 37: "The essence of
mechanical explanation, in fact, is to regard the future and the past
as calculable functions of the present, and thus to claim that *all is
given.*"

credit!'—these were some of his golden maxims,—'never take paper-money! Look well to your change.' " While Hepzibah is trying to digest these "hard little pellets" of wisdom, he advises her above all to put on the signet of the street, a "warm, sunny smile." The years of plodding up and down the gravel and pavement have left their mark on Uncle Venner's attire: he is patched together of different epochs, a veritable "epitome of times and fashions." Never having possessed the corrupting power of Judge Pyncheon, he is tough and vigorous without being hard. Sheer antiquity has mellowed him so that he is as familiar within several family circles as he is outside on the street. He looks forward with pathetic cheer to ending his days at his "farm"—the poorhouse. He is one of Hawthorne's few unforgettable minor characters.

Early in the first chapter Hawthorne cites the prediction that old Matthew Maule's ghost would haunt the "new apartments" of the Pyncheon house. This prophecy comes true in the person of Holgrave, who lives in "a remote gable" of the house, barred from the main portion. He dwells in the house only to learn how to hate it, for, as his chameleonic past indicates, his real home has been the street. His education has been the result of "passing through the thoroughfare of life"; among other trades, he has been a salesman and a traveling peddler. In his present occupation as daguerreotypist he makes pictures out of the street's element, the sunlight. But he is neither a man of patches like Uncle Venner nor an empty monument of fashion like Judge Pyncheon. His clothes—a simple inexpensive suit and clean linen—are an indication that he has retained his integrity despite past vicissitudes. He resembles the seeker for truth in "The Intelligence Office": "somewhat too rough-hewn and brawny for a scholar" and yet motivated by an intellectual curiosity of which his daguerreotypes are emblems. As Fogle has pointed out, his pictures lack depth and chiaroscuro. They penetrate Jaffrey's exterior but, like Holgrave's limited vision, offer no insight into the complex shadows of the house and its occupants; they abstract the particular individual from his context. Typical of many of his compeers, Holgrave has cut himself off from tradition, even to the extent of changing his name. Though he does not realize it at first, he is a man in search of roots. Beneath his shifting political beliefs and his varied occupations lies a yearning for stability.

Mediating between the dark house and the sunlit street is the little shop, "where the projection of the second story and the thick foliage of the elm-tree, as well as the commodities at the window, created a sort of *gray medium*." Catering chiefly to the juvenile trade, the shop forms a sequestered, childlike imitation of the grinding commerce in the street. A second spot where elements from the house and street converge is the garden. It provides a refuge from their stark realities and is a "green play-place of flickering light," where aristocratic flowers and plebeian vegetables, rank weeds and white rosebushes may intermingle. Here Holgrave and Uncle Venner, Clifford and Hepzibah may converse and watch undisturbed the "paltry rivulet of life." But the real mistress of both shop and garden is Phoebe. In the early part of the book she moves freely through house and street without being fully aware of their implications. Her room fronts on the garden while Holgrave's faces the street, but both the young people lack depth of vision. In her girlish innocence Phoebe sees nothing in Maule's well but the colored pebbles at the bottom.

The two massive symbols of house and street thus pervade the book, and the conflict between them sets the stage for its most memorable scenes. Hepzibah is introduced to us at the moment "when the patrician lady is to be transformed into the plebeian woman. . . . She must earn her own food, or starve" (III, 55). The urgent necessity for her to adapt herself to the brisk ways of the street is underscored by Hawthorne's grim reminder that "in this republican country, amid the fluctuating waves of our social life, somebody is always at the drowning-point." Her situation reminds us of the modern evolutionary doctrine that extinction is caused by a change in the organism-environment integration that requires the organism to make an adaptive change it is unable to make. As G. G. Simpson puts it, "When a group is already waning and approaching the danger of extinction, its local interbreeding populations eventually fall below the size where random, inadaptive mutations are regularly eliminated without becoming fixed in an undue proportion of the population. This, with accompanying excessive inbreeding also likely in such a situation, may tend to produce bizarre, sickly, or generally inadaptive forms."[7] Hepzibah, like her chickens, is such a bizarre and inadaptive form. But she is also and above all an indomitable human being, one who knows when to join, when to compromise, and when to fight. Her pathetic failure as an "aristocratic hucksteress" is overshadowed by her love for Clifford, her kindness to Phoebe, and her staunch resistance to the Judge.

If Hepzibah needs "a walk along the noonday street to keep her sane," Clifford requires an even greater shock. An inveterate conservative, he has more difficulty than she does in adjusting to the street. Alternately attracted and repelled by its incessant activity, he is baffled by such novelties as the omnibus, the water cart, and the train, all of which oppress him with "the idea of terrible energy." In his retrogressive condition, he finds himself most at home with the girlish

[7] Simpson, *The Meaning of Evolution,* p. 204.

Phoebe in the garden. To be reborn, he needs to immerse himself in the destructive element, "to take a deep, deep plunge into the ocean of human life, and to sink down and be covered by its profoundness, and then to emerge, sobered, invigorated, restored to the world and to himself." Enveloped in his damask dreams of the past, he makes two abortive gestures toward reunion with the life of the present: once when he nearly jumps from the window into the midst of a political procession and again when he and Hepzibah desperately strive to attend church.

The chapter describing Clifford's temporary but invigorating escape from the house is probably the high point of the book. Jaffrey's death seems to lift the whole burden of the past; Clifford excitedly throws off his damask dressing gown, dons a cloak, and triumphantly guides Hepzibah out of the house into the street. Almost instinctively, he guides her to a train, which as we have already noticed is one of Hawthorne's symbolic representations of the contemporary scene. As the train gathers speed and the landscape with its emblems of the past melts away in the gloom of the stormy afternoon, Clifford immediately adopts a marvelous hodgepodge of contemporary ideas. In an ironic parallel with Holgrave, he hysterically denounces the evils that accumulate around roof and hearthstone and urges their destruction by fire. With Emersonian optimism he describes evolution as an ever ascending spiral of progress in which material crudities are gradually spiritualized. "These railroads—could but the whistle be made musical, and the rumble and the jar got rid of—are positively the greatest blessing that the ages have wrought out for us," he says to a gimlet-eyed stranger. "They give us wings; they annihilate the toil and dust of pilgrimage; they spiritualize travel!" As further evidence that the world is growing ethereal, he cites the phenomena of mesmerism and spiritualism. His excitement grows to a feverish pitch when he exalts the vitalizing power of electricity. "Then there is electricity,—the demon, the angel, the mighty physical power, the all-pervading intelligence!" he exclaims. "Is it a fact—or have I dreamt it—that, by means of electricity, the world of matter has become a great nerve, vibrating thousands of miles in a breathless point of time? Rather, the round globe is a vast head, a brain, instinct with intelligence." These speculations, faintly reminiscent of *Naturphilosophie,* are climaxed by Clifford's praise of the telegraph, which, like Thoreau, he considers to be "an almost spiritual medium."

Clifford's new acquaintance is understandably bewildered by all this. But his parting comment, as the two wanderers prepare to alight from the train, unwittingly reveals one of the ironies attendant upon Clifford's paean to spiritualization. "I can't see through you!" the stranger says, pointing up the fact that Clifford's excursion into the world has given him an opacity inconsonant with his former shadowy status in the house.[8] This mood is temporary, however, for at the lonely train station Clifford and Hepzibah are confronted by two relics of the past—a wooden church "black with age" and a farmhouse "in the old style." Clifford's tremulous exhilaration bubbles away, and he turns once again to Hepzibah for guidance. Yet their trip has not been a total failure, for here on the isolated platform, lifting her hands to the dull, gray sky, Hepzibah is able to pray—something she has been unable to do in the house.

While the two fugitives are embarked on their wild flight through the street and Clifford is temporarily assuming its substantial veneer, the corpse of Judge Pyncheon gradually

[8] Here I am indebted to Clark Griffith, "Substance and Shadow: Language and Meaning in *The House of the Seven Gables," Modern Philology,* LI (February, 1954), 187–95.

fades into the shadows of the house. Throughout his life he has clutched at the solid "realities" of the past—the real estate—while shrugging off the intangible hereditary factors that contain his ultimate doom. On the surface (and this, of course, is as far as his self-analysis would go), his motives are clear. Clifford has been released from prison through the Judge's political influence; he will either divulge the whereabouts of the map or Jaffrey will have him declared insane. Yet from the start, when Hepzibah opens her shop and the Judge scrutinizes the house from "the opposite side" of the street, one feels that his efforts to get inside the house subconsciously stem from something deeper than greed. He must exorcize that black dram of evil which, a few hours of the year, keeps overbalancing all his good works; he must wrench out and analyze the secret of the interior. Though this obsession is never made explicit, Hepzibah hints at it when she tells him, "mournfully, not passionately," that "it is you that are diseased in mind, not Clifford!" The macabre chapter in which Hawthorne gloats over the Judge's death has repelled some modern tastes. But it climaxes the subtle interaction between space and time that permeates the book. One of the massive ironies in the Judge's demise lies in the distinction between abstract and real time. As we have noted, he has been a devotee of the mechanical system in which time is measured spatially. It is a knife-edge point of view that assumes that our experience takes place at discrete instants. The essence of this attitude, as Bergson observed, is "to regard the future and the past as calculable functions of the present, and thus to claim that all is given." The little card that falls out of Jaffrey's pocket on the doorstep forms "a prospective epitome of the day's history"; his unerringly accurate watch has measured the distance between his various engagements. One might say, indeed, that the Judge's

Evolution and Regeneration: The House of the Seven Gables

watch has replaced his pulse. But now, in the darkening inner parlor of the house, both watch and pulse run down; the Judge is overwhelmed by real time; "the great world-clock of Time still keeps its beat." Hawthorne compresses the outcome in one sarcastic pun: "Time, all at once, appears to have become a matter of no moment with the Judge!"

The rhetoric of this chapter is not just a showpiece; it functions as part of the irony. The house, as we have noted, is the custodian of the word: it holds the documents, books, and poetry from the past. Now, in his gross material fashion, the Judge has tried to effect the kind of synthesis of the Light and the Word in the Act that we examined in *The Scarlet Letter*. He has always possessed plenty of light and considerable oily eloquence, but he feels the need of the old word— the document—and the act, that is, the "deed." The attempt kills him.[9] Hawthorne buries this creature of modern sunshine and festive eloquence under seventeenth-century rhetoric. The devices of Petrus Ramus and the slogans of the Puritans come back to haunt Jaffrey Pyncheon:

Rise up, Judge Pyncheon! The morning sunshine glimmers through the foliage, and, beautiful and holy as it is, shuns not to kindle up your face. Rise up, thou subtle, worldly, selfish, iron-hearted hypocrite, and make thy choice whether still to be subtle, worldly, selfish, iron-hearted, and hypocritical, or to tear these sins out of thy nature, though they bring the life-blood with them! The Avenger is upon thee! Rise up, before it be too late!

The metamorphosis of Phoebe and Holgrave is less effective than that of Clifford, Hepzibah, and Jaffrey. One rea-

[9] Alfred H. Marks has convincingly argued that Judge Pyncheon was frightened to death by the ghostlike Clifford, who embodied the values of the imagination. See "Who Killed Judge Pyncheon? The Role of the Imagination in *The House of the Seven Gables,*" *Publications of the Modern Language Association,* LXXI (June, 1956), 355–69.

son for this is that they initially possess so many good traits that not much change is necessary for them to attain moral balance. As Holgrave's story of Alice Pyncheon shows, the development of the Pyncheons and the Maules may in some instances be morally progressive. Phoebe has Alice's beauty and her love of music without her arrogance; Holgrave possesses Matthew Maule's hypnotic powers but, unlike his ancestor, reveres the individuality of others. Hawthorne's problem is to portray the gradual maturation of his young couple. With Phoebe he is not very successful; we are told that her association with the house has made her less girlish, more a woman, but we do not feel it.

Holgrave's growth, though it is perhaps too rapid to be credible, is more interesting because it is partly unfolded through the action. The worst aspect of his "oscillating tendency" appears when Hepzibah, confronted by the inexorable Judge, seeks aid in defending Clifford. Her thoughts naturally turn to Holgrave, who might well become "the champion of a crisis." But when she unlocks the door to his room, she discovers that he is not there. At the time when he is needed most, the daguerreotypist is "at his public rooms." Later, however, after he has spent a miserable, lonely hour with Jaffrey's body, Holgrave discovers the reality of duration, of guilt and retribution, and in doing so discovers himself.

Hawthorne wrote to Evert Duyckinck that he had intended to bring *The House of the Seven Gables* to a "prosperous close."[10] By this he probably meant that he had attempted to reconcile the values of past and present in a "sunny" ending. But when he reached this point, he was apparently unable or unwilling to take the proposed reconciliation serious-

[10] The letter is quoted in Eleanor Melville Metcalf, *Herman Melville: Cycle and Epicycle* (Harvard University Press, Cambridge, Mass., 1953), pp. 102–104.

Evolution and Regeneration: The House of the Seven Gables

ly, and the final pages degenerate into flimsy farce. Good old Uncle Venner, it turns out, is not going to end his days in the poorhouse but will dwell in a little gingerbread cottage at the country estate. (Chanticleer and his hens have already moved there and have begun an indefatigable orgy of egg-laying.) Holgrave, having completely surrendered to Phoebe, is contemplating do-it-yourself projects, including a cut-stone house in suburbia. Hepzibah, now worth a couple of hundred thousand dollars, is prodigal in her gifts. Maule's well, formerly notable for its profound depths, is now vomiting up a succession of kaleidoscopic pictures. The whole conclusion is summed up in a vision of Alice Pyncheon floating to heaven on her harp.

The feeble ending is, perhaps, as E. M. Forster has suggested, a defect inherent in the novel form, and Hawthorne's failure here does not seriously lessen his solid achievement in the book. Unlike *The Scarlet Letter,* which is pure tragedy, *The House of the Seven Gables* is tragicomedy. Less intense than the earlier book, it is more massive in its carefully selected realistic detail and its structure. The lapse of two centuries between Colonel Pyncheon and the present generation provides Hawthorne with a deep well of concealed activity from which he can draw at will. He pulls the reader into this past by constant allusion and by the deliberate distortion of straightforward narrative in Chapter XXII. The main structural element is the contrast between the house and the street, which forms an arched window, as it were, through which we view the moral evolution of the Pyncheons. At the apex of the arch are the two chapters in which Clifford and Jaffrey simultaneously invade alien domains: whereas Clifford hails the annihilation of time, Jaffrey is engulfed by it; while Clifford emerges into the Light, Jaffrey is buried under the Word. By juxtaposing these two chapters

HAWTHORNE'S TRAGIC VISION

Hawthorne temporarily halts the time flow of the narrative and concentrates our attention upon the ironic correlation of the events of one stormy afternoon. The result is a structural emphasis upon the book's theme—the interpenetration of the past and the present.

viii —

The Pastoral Wasteland:
The Blithedale Romance

I~N~ *The Blithedale Romance* (1852) Hawthorne arrived at his definitive criticism of the recurring American efforts at transformation without tragedy. While his ever optimistic contemporaries were busy converting trees into lumber, whales into oil, and water into power, Hawthorne adhered to his "one idea": that moral conversion, which is the only kind that really matters, cannot be achieved through intellectual schemes, incessant industry, or technological progress. A spiritual sea change must be *suffered;* this is unfortunate, but there is no other way. "There is no instance in all history," he wrote in his life of Pierce, "of the human will and intellect having perfected any great moral reform by methods which it adapted to that end" (XII, 417).

With this central idea in mind, Hawthorne composed *The Blithedale Romance* by selecting and manipulating his observations and experiences of a decade: the gruesome suicide of a woman in the prime of life; the contemporary delusion of mesmerism; the Brook Farm experiment; the quiet, determined drinkers at Parker's grogshop; the gulf between the intellectual and the yeoman; his interest in the dangerously sterile but fascinating role of the withdrawn observer. In 1842 he set down one hint of the story to come when he wrote in his notebook: "To allegorize life with a masquerade, and represent mankind generally as masquers. Here and there a natural face may appear." The vision of life that emerged ten years later, though it lacks the tense conflict of *The Scarlet Letter*, is far richer than one usually realizes upon first reading. The book seems to me to be perfectly achieved and just as relevant in the age of extrasensory perception and atomic conversion as it was in the era of mesmerism. Until recently, criticism of *The Blithedale Romance* so often dwelled upon such peripheral matters as whether or not Zenobia resembled Margaret Fuller that it remains one of the most underrated works in American fiction.[1]

Now that the demands for a prosaic realism in fiction have receded, it is unnecessary to labor the point that *The Blithedale Romance* is not an ineffectual effort at a documentary of Brook Farm, nor is it merely Hawthorne's satirical comment on philanthropists and reform movements. As he stated in

[1] Extremes of critical opinion were summarized by Frank Davidson in an article that also contributed a valuable analysis of the book's pervasive veil imagery: "Toward a Revaluation of *The Blithedale Romance*," *New England Quarterly*, XXV (September, 1952), 374–83. See also Fogle, *Hawthorne's Fiction*, pp. 140–61; Waggoner, *Hawthorne*, pp. 174–94.

the preface and in a letter to G.W. Curtis, the real subject of the book is neither Brook Farm nor socialism. His work presents, as Henry James would say, "experience liberated, so to speak; experience disengaged, disembroiled, disencumbered, exempt from the conditions which usually attach to it," so that its deepest implications may be explored. The implications in this instance are not pleasant to contemplate, but to a generation educated by D. H. Lawrence, T. S. Eliot, Thomas Mann, and Robert Penn Warren they probably seem more real than they did in 1852. The Blithedale community stands as the type of all those efforts in the Western world to ignore Solomon's wisdom about the seasons, to purify by escaping from time into space, to achieve rebirth by putting on a mask. The comic masquerade, as Hawthorne viewed it, is the mode of changing our minds, and as such it is vitally necessary. The mischief comes when we expect it to change our hearts.

Blithedale, then, turns out to be an ironic name, thinly veiling what ultimately emerges as a pastoral wasteland. The inhabitants of the community debate over a name for their utopia; some favor calling it "The Oasis," but "others insisted on a proviso for reconsidering the matter at a twelve-month's end, when a final decision might be had, whether to name it 'The Oasis,' or 'Sahara'." By the end of the book it is obvious that Blithedale, far from being "the one green spot in the moral sand-waste of the world," has instead simply revealed its own barrenness. What the inhabitants hope will be a May Day—a warm, "hearty" purification—turns out to be a winter's tale told in retrospect by a frosty bachelor.

Hawthorne deliberately wrote, I suspect, toward the "big scene" that he felt to be securely within his grasp—the midnight discovery of Zenobia's suicide. Soon after the story opens, to cite but one instance, Zenobia prophesies her fate with "the entrance of the sable knight Hollingsworth and this shadowy snow-maiden, who, precisely at the stroke of midnight, shall melt away at my feet in a pool of ice-cold water and give me my death with a pair of wet slippers." Coverdale's dream, in which he foresees "a dim shadow" of the catastrophe, thus provides an explicit comment on Hawthorne's method of subtly anticipating later events.

The Blithedale experiment is, first, an attempt to avoid the embrace of time. Coverdale and his friends ride "far beyond the strike of city clocks" into pure, snow-covered space. Theirs is an effort to blur the distinction between seasons, to overcome the desolation of winter by the warmth of their reforming zeal. "We can never call ourselves regenerated men," says one of Coverdale's companions, "till a February northeaster shall be as grateful to us as the softest breeze of June" (V, 333). They declare May Day a "movable festival," and it is only the ineffectual Coverdale who gradually senses the blank unreality of their "spick-and-span novelty." By the time he decides to leave the community, he has finally attained a wisdom that, though commonplace elsewhere, seems downright orphic after life at Blithedale: "Times change, and people change," he tells Priscilla; "and if our hearts do not change as readily, so much the worse for us" (V, 483).

Acting as a measure of the community's failure, therefore, is the temporal structure of the book. Narrated by one who has withdrawn from life, the story unfolds against the background of the seasons.[2] Viewed against the fundamental rhythms of nature, the various human efforts at rebirth without roots become even more frustrating. Recalling the firelight, which at the beginning of the Blithedale experiment

[2] Fogle has pointed out that the seasons are an important element in the structure. *Hawthorne's Fiction*, pp. 141–42.

had made the men look "full of youth, warm blood, and hope," Coverdale ruefully remarks that its genial glow has now dwindled to the "phosphoric glimmer . . . which exudes . . . from the damp fragments of decayed trees." He explicitly proclaims his own rebirth in May: having passed through a kind of death, he is "quite another man," "clothed anew." And later he finds a "hermitage" in the weeds that suggests the perfect shelter of the womb. It is "a hollow chamber of rare seclusion" in which his individuality is "inviolate." Sitting there, Coverdale prophesies a rebirth in October: "I . . . fore-reckoned the abundance of my vintage. It gladdened me to anticipate the surprise of the Community when, like an allegorical figure of rich October, I should make my appearance, with shoulders bent beneath the burden of ripe grapes and some of the crushed ones crimsoning my brows with a blood-stain." But this fruitful October never comes for him, and in the end he is forced to acknowledge that his life has been "all an emptiness."

There are other futile attempts at regeneration. The drinkers in the saloon achieve "renewed youth and vigor, the brisk, cheerful sense of things present and to come"—a feeling that lasts "for about a quarter of an hour." The fate of these people is typified in the picture of a drunkard that hangs on the wall. "The death-in-life was too well portrayed. . . . Your only comfort lay in the forced reflection, that real as he looked, the poor caitiff was but imaginary—a bit of painted canvas." The mesmerist, Westervelt, also offers a new life. He speaks of "a new era that was dawning upon the world; an era that would link soul to soul with a closeness that should finally convert both worlds into one great, mutually conscious brotherhood." The "cold and dead materialism" of this brotherhood is matched by the mechanical method of conversion advocated by Fourier. Drain the salt from the sea, as he had proposed, transform the water to lemonade, and all the savor is gone. *The Blithedale Romance* is thus a kind of *Walden* in reverse. (Zenobia, coincidentally, anticipates Thoreau's exact words when she says of her experience in the community: "It was good; but there are other lives as good or better.") The story begins in the spring and ends with the fall; the whole progression is condensed in the exhilaration of the brisk September day that makes Coverdale buoyant at first but later only emphasizes his "sickness of the spirits."

The effort to reform the spirit externally, then, leads to disintegration. Sharply contrasted to the dynamic wholeness of nature are the images of rigidity, mutilation, and decay that lead inexorably to the discovery of Zenobia's horribly rigid and mutilated corpse. It is "the marble image of a death-agony," the catastrophe that Coverdale dimly foresaw when he awakened from his dream after the first evening in Blithedale and saw the moon shining on the snowy land-scape, which looked "like a lifeless copy of the world in marble." Zenobia is cast aside like "a broken tool" by the inflexible Hollingsworth; and Coverdale's cool analysis of Hollingsworth is, as he himself admits, a kind of dissection. "If we take the freedom to put a friend under our microscope," he says, "we inevitably tear him into bits." The Blithedale group is "gentility in tatters," while the visitors from town, the ratlike Moodie and the infamous Westervelt, embody a decadent materialism. The mesmerist's discourse is like "a current of chill air issuing out of a sepulchral vault, and bringing the smell of corruption along with it."

The second major pattern of images is one of withdrawal and concealment. As Frank Davidson has pointed out, everyone in the book except Silas Foster and his pigs is veiled in one form or another. Priscilla, the Veiled Lady, is "insulated" from time and space; the pseudonym of Zenobia is a "sort of mask in which she comes from the world, retaining all the privileges of privacy—a contrivance, in short, like the white drapery of the Veiled Lady." Old Moodie hides behind his alias and his patch; Westervelt's gold teeth reveal him to Coverdale as a humbug whose "face, for aught I knew, might be removable like a mask." Hollingsworth's mask is his philanthropic project: "You are a better masquerader than the witches and gypsies yonder," Zenobia tells him, "for your disguise is a self-deception." The whole community has, of course, withdrawn from life into a kind of masquerade, but Coverdale finds it necessary to retreat even further into the hermitage. His typical stance finds him "a little withdrawn from the window."

The failure of Blithedale may be summed up as a misplaced faith in the comic vision of life as a mode of emotional conversion. The essence of the comic vision, as Hawthorne considered it, lay in the breaking of bonds—links with the past, ties with social classes. As Melville's mentor Solomon said, there is "a time to embrace, and a time to refrain from embracing," and the communitarians have confused the tragic usefulness of the one with the comic purpose of the other. Their neighbors highlight this confusion in their comments.

They told slanderous fables about our inability to yoke our own oxen, or to drive them afield when yoked, or to release the poor brutes from their conjugal bond at nightfall. They had the face to say, too, that the cows laughed at our awkwardness at milking-time, and invariably kicked over the pails; partly in consequence of our putting the stool on the wrong side. . . . They further averred that . . . by dint of unskillful planting few of our seeds ever came up at all, or if they did come up it was stern-foremost. . . . Finally, and as an ultimate catastrophe, these mendacious

rogues circulated a report that we communitarians were extermi-
nated, to the last man, by severing ourselves asunder, with the
sweep of our own scythes!

As in *The Scarlet Letter,* our understanding of what Hawthorne is doing in this book hinges in part upon accurate
identification of the characters and the allegorical personifications. Once again we find the woman (Zenobia) and the
man (Hollingsworth), their guilt (Westervelt), and their
possible redemption (Priscilla). But here the woman is attempting to evade the "one event" of womanhood; the man
has welded an intellectual shield over his heart; the redemptive agent is the medium of both truth and falsehood; and
the story is narrated in the first person by an observer.

The most vital character in the book is Zenobia. The very
essence of womanhood, she is the "first comer," she is the
Amazon queen, she is Eve. "One felt an influence breathing
out of her," says Coverdale, "such as we might suppose to
come from Eve, when she was first made, and her creator
brought her to Adam, saying, 'Behold! here is a woman!'"
And he cannot resist summoning up a vision of her, clad in
"Eve's earliest garment."

Zenobia's present attire expresses her contempt for the
traditional role of women. As Newton Arvin observed some
years ago, her exotic flower indicates her pride in competing
with men. She desires to go afield, to speculate; just as she
has no scruples about rifling a cherry tree of its blossoms, so
her full flowering will be cut off by her attempt to be "stump-
oratress." She despises the traditional feminine occupation
of investment; this sympathetic function has been split off
and concentrated in the seamstress, Priscilla. Like all Hawthorne's women (as opposed to his feminine personifications), Zenobia's character has "good and evil in it." Redun-

dant with life, she makes all the other characters seem pale. But in this pastoral wasteland, her vitality is doomed. The others are bent upon destroying it: Coverdale by his incessant probing, his cool dissection, and Hollingsworth by making her a tool in his conspiracy. But it is Zenobia herself who is chiefly responsible for her self-destruction. She is quite willing to subvert the most gracious aspects of her womanhood (Priscilla) in order to have Hollingsworth on her own terms.

When man attempts to purify himself through psychiatry, intellectual schemes, and material progress, the burden of guilt tends to assume the very forms by which he seeks to erase it. Thus Zenobia's guilt is embodied in Westervelt, who, as his name implies, speaks with "the tone of worldly society at large." The "moral deterioration attendant on a false and shallow life" that results from Zenobia's "marriage" to the values of the Western world inevitably leads to her death beneath the dark mask of the river. When Coverdale sees her in the luxurious boardinghouse, she has taken on a glittering luster that, like her flower, is artificial. Even her death has something affected about it: Coverdale observes that "we cannot even put ourselves to death in whole-hearted simplicity."

The gradual destruction of Zenobia is reinforced, as we have noted, by images that shift from life to death. The death images are combined in the personification of her guilt. Westervelt's appearance at the lyceum is the nadir in a series of morbid exhibitions; he is preceded by the physiologist with his "real skeletons" and by the museum of wax figures. But what makes Westervelt completely repulsive is that he typifies a ghastly life-in-death. In his grim correlation of gold with mesmerism, Hawthorne anticipated Lionel Trilling's observation that money is like a spook in having a life of its own that properly it should not have. Like the stones in the house of Usher, Westervelt has an indecent, clammy existence. Coverdale's reaction to him is "a creeping of the flesh, as when feeling about in a dark place, one touches something cold and slimy." Westervelt's discourse at the lyceum reminds one of the metallic clanking as Madeline Usher rises from her underground vault.

As Zenobia says in her own defense, the major reason for her dissatisfaction with womanhood lies in the reduced stature of the man. "Let man be but manly and godlike," she tells Hollingsworth, "and woman is only too ready to become to him what you say." Originally warmhearted, close to the center of humanity, he has become the false priest of this "apostolic society." Unexpectedly tender in caring for the invalid Coverdale and unique in the community in possessing a strong religious faith, Hollingsworth can manage everyone but himself. He preaches eloquently from Eliot's pulpit to his three "disciples," but his abstract desire to root out all evil becomes merely a shield to protect himself from healthy emotion. The dangers of his abstraction appear most clearly in his "visionary edifice." Instead of planning a home with roots, a house that would be "time-worn, and full of storied love, and joy, and sorrow," he tries to seduce the woman into inhabiting a purely intellectual prison for "the reform and mental culture of our criminal brethren." In masquerading as a reformer, Hollingsworth deceives not only his friends but also himself. When he finally attains self-knowledge, it is too late for any fruitful union with the woman. Recognizing his fatal error in rejecting the vitality of Zenobia and his part in her death, he condemns himself to an agony of self-accusation. His final outcome cannot be fully understood, however, until we grasp Priscilla's identity.

As Hawthorne's opening introduction of the Veiled Lady

The Pastoral Wasteland: The Blithedale Romance

would indicate, Priscilla is a key figure in the story, though as a personification her chief importance proceeds from her relationships to other characters. Various clues help to establish her allegorical identity. An orphan in worldly society, linked only to the woman as stepsister and handmaiden, Priscilla is like Pearl in being the providential "first-fruits of the world." In commercial life she has been like a flower faintly blooming in the crack of a sidewalk. She has the gift of hearing the Miltonic "airy tongues that syllable forth men's names." No one from the town calls for her. Like Puck, she ruins the milk and spoils the dinner (V, 104). Priscilla, in short, is spritelike Fancy, the "medium" of truth and falsehood. Coverdale clearly identifies her during his illness. "There is a species of intuition," he says, "either a spiritual life, or the subtle recognition of a fact" that comes to us during sickness. "Vapors then rise up to the brain, and take shapes that often image falsehood, but sometimes truth" (V, 373). A few pages later, he remarks of Priscilla's visit to his bedside: "My weakly condition, I suppose, supplied a medium in which she could approach me" (V, 377). As the medium, Priscilla's charm is not "positive" or "material"; she is blown about like a leaf. "I never have any free will," she exclaims plaintively to Coverdale. Unable to stand on her own legs, she draws her potential life from Zenobia and Hollingsworth. As the artistic medium, her province lies "somewhere between disease and beauty." We see now why Hawthorne begins with the Veiled Lady. For the book's action may be summed up in the efforts of each character to manipulate, corrupt, or achieve the medium of truth.

Incidentally, Hawthorne uses Priscilla as his own medium for what I take to be a covert but devastating thrust at Margaret Fuller. Priscilla brings a "sealed letter" to Coverdale's bedside. When he does not immediately offer to take it,

Priscilla draws back and holds the letter "against her bosom, with both hands clasped over it." As she holds this pose, Miles is struck by a remarkable parallel. Though her figure and facial features differ, Priscilla's air and general expression remind him of "a friend of mine, one of the most gifted women of the age." A woman with a letter clasped to her bosom? Surely this is a veiled reference to Hester Prynne— an old friend of Hawthorne's and one of the most gifted women of any age. When Coverdale goes on to say that Priscilla reminds him of Margaret Fuller, we see that this is more than mild coincidence. The Transcendentalist authoress is being compared to the lady with the scarlet *A*; but where Hester's letter was "open," Margaret Fuller's is sealed. Whether this is simply Hawthorne's implied criticism of Miss Fuller's feminist activities or whether it is a more pointed comment on her personal life must be left to conjecture. All that he will say is that the comparison is "a singular anomaly of likeness coexisting with perfect dissimilitude" (V, 378).

Less important allegorically but more interesting as a person than Priscilla is Miles Coverdale, the middle-aged bachelor who tells the story in retrospect. He represents Hawthorne's sole full-length effort at rigorously limiting the point of view to a first-person narrator. A minor poet of the Transcendental school, Coverdale is a fictive ancestor of the cynical narrator, Jack Burden, in Robert Penn Warren's *All the King's Men*. A perceptive observer, he functions like Burden as the equivalent of a Greek chorus. It used to be argued that he was not sufficiently dissociated from the author; many of his experiences stem from those Hawthorne recorded in his notebook, and at times the narrator expresses views that we know to be those of his creator. But, as Matthiessen has cautioned in his *American Renaissance*, "We

The Pastoral Wasteland: The Blithedale Romance

must remember that Coverdale is not Hawthorne any more than Prufrock is Eliot, that in each case the author has exorcized a dangerous part of his experience by treating it with irony."[3] The simplest way to state the relationship is to say that Coverdale is what Hawthorne feared he might have become had he not given himself in love and marriage. But further modifications will have to be made as we examine Coverdale's role more closely.

His name, like the names Westervelt and Zenobia, was not chosen idly. It would be interesting to know Hawthorne's source of information about the sixteenth-century translator of the Bible, Miles Coverdale. It seems to have been fairly common knowledge that Coverdale was "somewhat weak and timorous, and all through his life leaned on a more powerful nature. In the hour of trouble he was content to remain in obscurity and left the crown of martyrdom to be earned by men of tougher stripe."[4] One could hardly ask for a better brief description of Hawthorne's minor poet.

Though Coverdale owes his name to the early sixteenth century, his predicament is eminently modern. Hawthorne himself knew only too well the dangers of retreating from life and the difficulty of opening up an intercourse with the world. In this book he objectified his experience by means of technique; that is, he discovered in the one major hazard of first-person narration a means for dramatizing the plight of his artist. As Percy Lubbock said in his classic study of the subject, when the point of view is limited, "the man or woman who acts as the vessel of sensation is always in danger of seeming a light, uncertain weight compared with the other people in the book—simply because the other people

---

[3] Matthiessen, *American Renaissance*, p. 229.
[4] Lacking a probable source from Hawthorne's reading, I quote from the *Dictionary of National Biography*.

are objective images, plainly outlined, while the seer in the midst is precluded from that advantage, and must see without being directly seen. He, who doubtless ought to bulk in the story more massively than anyone, tends to remain the least recognizable of the company, and even to dissolve in a kind of impalpable blur."[5] Coverdale ultimately admits that his life is "colorless," that he is but a "dim figure." The subject of *The Blithedale Romance* is thus inseparable from its form: the images of withdrawal and the traits of the narrator coincide with the way the story is told.

Coverdale's great fault, of course, is that he tries to live by proxy. (This may be the relevance of Priscilla's name; in New England's legendary history, the classic attempt to make love by proxy is associated with the names Miles and Priscilla.) He tries to know himself by probing the selves of others, and he accepts nothing on faith. Zenobia emphasizes this failing in her legend of the Veiled Lady. The Theodore of her story, like Coverdale, has "a natural tendency toward scepticism," and he conceals himself behind a screen. He will not take the Veiled Lady on faith; he prefers "to lift the veil first," just as Coverdale does with all his friends.

A bachelor with a taste for wine and a good cigar, Coverdale would be willing to die for a good cause—"provided, however, the effort did not involve an unreasonable amount of trouble. If Kossuth, for example, would pitch the battlefield of Hungarian rights within an easy ride of my abode, and choose a mild, sunny morning, after breakfast, for the conflict, Miles Coverdale would be his man, for one brave rush upon the levelled bayonets." It is not surprising that he finds it relatively easy to see the world through the eyes of

[5] Extracts from Percy Lubbock, *The Craft of Fiction*, reprinted as "The Strategy of Point of View," in *Critiques and Essays on Modern Fiction*, ed. John W. Aldridge (The Ronald Press Company, New York, 1952), p. 13.

the former hedonist, Moodie, and the cynical materialist, Westervelt. Like the painted old man who confronts Gustav von Aschenbach in Thomas Mann's *Death in Venice,* old Moodie is an image of Coverdale's future self. "I tried to identify my mind with the old fellow's," he says, "and take his view of the world, as if looking through a smoke-blackened glass at the sun. It robbed the landscape of all its life. . . . When my eyes are dimmer than they have yet come to be, I will go thither again, and see . . . if the cold and life-less tint of his perceptions be not then repeated in my own." The colorless Moodie, who lives solely in his daughters, pro-vides the book's most notable example of life by proxy and is thus Hawthorne's most incisive comment on Coverdale's weakness.

We sympathize with Coverdale partly because he resem-bles the modern intellectual cut off from ancient certitudes, longing to submerge himself in a group yet fearful that in doing so he will lose his individuality. Hollingsworth offers him a chance to submit to authority in an effort to benefit humanity. His appeal is very similar to that of the Com-munist party when it attracted numerous intellectuals in the nineteen thirties, or to that of the Church in earlier cen-turies: "It [Hollingsworth's project] offers you (what you have told me, over and over again, that you most need) a purpose in life, worthy of the extremest self-devotion,—worthy of martyrdom, should God so order it! In this view, I present it to you. You can greatly benefit mankind. Your peculiar faculties, as I shall direct them, are capable of being so wrought into this enterprise that not one of them need lie idle." This impulse toward authoritarianism, when coupled with the intimate personal bond between the two men, makes Hollingsworth's proposal almost irresistible. "Be with me . . . or be against me," he says, with the either-or logic of the demagogue. "There is no third choice for you." Despite this pressure, Coverdale retains his integrity; for once he reserves the right to look "through his own optics." But even this, his one great moral triumph, is, typically, an act of rejection.

Miles Coverdale ought to be a translator, like his sixteenth-century prototype. But one of the book's recurrent ironies is that during the empty religious experience of this small army of "saints and martyrs" no translation—moral or artistic—occurs. Priscilla knits her silk purses, and Silas Foster tends his swine; but she is remarkably inefficient in the farm routine, and he is simply bored with intellectual or artistic endeavors. Thus the book demonstrates the impossibility of making a silk purse out of a sow's ear. Coverdale recognizes that his poetry is thin and bodiless, but he is so exhausted by his raw experience that he is unable to convert it into art. This, we know, was often Hawthorne's view of his own artistic predicament, both in America at the customhouse and later in England at the consulate. But he was never driven to Coverdale's final position of proclaiming an acutely self-conscious art for art's sake. Coverdale has earlier remarked that he cared for Priscilla—not for her realities but for "the fancy-work with which I have idly decked her out" (V, 434). With no vital content in his art, he becomes solipsistically obsessed with its form. Thus at the end of the book he feebly confesses his love for his medium.

Priscilla, as we know, has been wedded to Hollingsworth. He is united with the medium of truth only after he has been educated by Zenobia's death. As Hawthorne put it a few years later, "Woman must strike through her own heart to reach a human life" (VI, 61). In *The Scarlet Letter* and *The Marble Faun* this tragic awareness proceeds from a passion-

The Pastoral Wasteland: The Blithedale Romance

ate union between man and woman. But in *The Blithedale Romance* there is no redemption through tragedy—only an abortive catastrophe. In their quest for reformation and refinement, the man and woman of the Western world have sacrificed their normal emotions, including sexual passion. Coverdale hints at the sexless outcome of their relationship when he anticipates a "sufficiently tragic catastrophe, though the dagger and the bowl should go for nothing in it" (V, 410). The sexual imagery is fully developed in the gruesome midnight search for Zenobia's body, when Hollingsworth with "a nervous jerky movement" begins to plunge his hooked pole into the blackness and eventually penetrates Zenobia's heart. The implication seems to be that once the normal rhythms of time, the seasons, and love are rejected, they will reassert themselves in ugly distorted forms. Coverdale had earlier remarked that Blithedale "seemed to authorize any individual, of either sex, to fall in love with any other, regardless of what would elsewhere be judged suitable and prudent" (V, 401). What begins as pastoral love play ends in what might almost be called necrophilia.

The Blithedale Romance is thus Hawthorne's most pessimistic book. It is pessimistic precisely because the characters attain no tragic vision. Between the routine, mechanized time of the city clocks and the dynamic, natural seasons lies Blithedale—"an epoch of annihilated space." Between "the conservatives, the writers of 'The North American Review,' the merchants, the politicians, the Cambridge men, and all those respectable old blockheads, who still . . . kept a death-grip on one or two ideas which had not come into vogue since yesterday morning" and the unsubstantial globe of Blithedale lies a vacuum for Coverdale, a dark watery grave for Zenobia, and an eternity of agonizing reappraisal for

HAWTHORNE'S TRAGIC VISION

Hollingsworth. As D. H. Lawrence perceived, Hawthorne knew "disagreeable things in his inner soul." Many of these things have been rediscovered in this century. But we have produced few novelists who can write of them not only with Hawthorne's unflinching courage but with his warm, deep sympathy.

ix ~

The Transfiguration of Figures:
The Marble Faun

MANY READERS, even those who appreciate
Hawthorne's other works, have found
The Marble Faun slow going. Its defects as a novel have
often been observed.[1] No coherent structure is immediately
apparent; particularly in the opening chapters, Hawthorne
is guilty of awkward transitions and clumsily playful author-
to-reader comments; the narrative seems to bog down in the
lengthy descriptions of Rome and its art objects. Of the four
characters, only Miriam and Donatello show any signs of

---

[1] See Waggoner, *Hawthorne*, pp. 201–207; Mark Van Doren, *Haw-*
thorne (William Sloane Associates, New York, 1949), pp. 226–30.

vitality. To make matters worse, Hawthorne teases the reader into looking at the wrong side of the tapestry; he supplies clues about Miriam and the model, for instance, that prompt precisely the kind of investigation he deplores in the conclusion.

The book's almost complete failure as novel inevitably limits its worth as romance, and I think *The Marble Faun* must finally be reckoned the least successful of Hawthorne's finished works. Yet with all its defects, the book deserves a sympathetic rereading, since its complex framework embraces Hawthorne's fullest explorations of morality and art. Indeed, its shortcomings result mainly from the grandeur of his aim. Never before had he tried to achieve so much in his medium; never before had he pressed the romance to its breaking point, as he does with Hilda in this book. His own comments reflect this gap between achievement and goal. "The thing is a failure," he said, in a mood of despair; yet he also called *The Marble Faun* his "best work."

Hawthorne's subject, once again, is the "riddle of the soul's growth" (VI, 434). How does man develop his full human potential? How do incarnation, conversion, transfiguration take place? The central figures in this process are already familiar to us: the young man who frolics in timeless spatial freedom and innocence; the woman inexorably linked with time and guilt but also with a redemptive ideal; and the union between them, with its attendant shocks and recognitions. In *The House of the Seven Gables* Hawthorne involved the individual with his immediate cultural and familial ancestry; here he plunges the innocent into all time, confronts him with the totality of the past and with the very "model," the prototype of evil.

Some of Hawthorne's difficulties resulted from his efforts to achieve a density he felt to be lacking in his earlier work.

The Transfiguration of Figures: The Marble Faun

In this book he strove to make the observer-commentator, Kenyon, a more substantial figure than Miles Coverdale; he tried to make Hilda both an allegorical ideal and a character; and he aimed at fusing action and setting in a structure more complex than any he had hitherto attempted. In this last intention he was quite successful, though the book's structure is discernible only after careful reading.

As the opening and concluding chapters indicate, the book is about four characters—Miriam, Hilda, Kenyon, and Donatello—who undergo a threefold process of transformation. The simplest way of grasping the book's structure is to envisage a circle divided into four parts revolving about a center. This center, or central experience, is expressed in various ways throughout the book. It is the way of conversion, in art and in life. Hawthorne discerns a "threefold analogy,—the clay model, the Life; the plaster cast, the Death; and the sculptured marble, the Resurrection" (VI, 432). Indeed, all of Rome itself seems designed after this analogy. Its grimy streets swarm with intricate, colorful life; its pavements cover a grave; and its towers and churches stretch heavenward. "Everywhere . . . a Cross,—and nastiness at the foot of it" (VI, 135).

The history of Rome and its environs follows the same pattern. The first stage was the innocent "sylvan life of Etruria, while Italy was yet guiltless of Rome"; the second was the sin and fall of Rome; the third, of course, was the rise of Christianity from the labyrinthine depths of the fall. These three periods are marked by cultural "peaks": Etruria in the Faun of Praxiteles in Chapter I; Rome in the statue of Marcus Aurelius in Chapter XVIII (which is entitled "On the Edge of the Precipice" and concludes with the "fall" of the model and of Donatello); and Christianity in the statue of Pope Julius in Chapter XXXV.

To combine the four characters and the threefold process is to arrive at the mystic number seven, which receives much attention in the book. The seven-branched candlestick that was lost at the Ponte Moll during Constantine's reign suggests to Hilda "an admirable idea for a mystic story or parable, or seven-branched allegory, full of poetry, art, philosophy, and religion (VI, 422). The whole ritual of transformation is summed up in Miriam's bridal gift to Hilda, an Etruscan bracelet, "the connecting bond of a series of seven wondrous tales, all of which, as they were dug out of seven sepulchres, were characterized by a seven-fold sepulchral gloom." In its "entire circle," the bracelet is the symbol of a "sad mystery," though there is a gleam of hope at the end.

In someone else's fiction we might dismiss these recurrent allusions to a seven-branched allegory as idle fancy, but Hawthorne seldom if ever labors a point unless it has meaning. Looking back over the book, we discover that every seventh chapter contains a recognition scene in which an individual is transfigured by a vital bond with the past. These sacramental "rites" do not follow the orthodox order prescribed by the Roman Catholics, nor do we expect them to. What Hawthorne does insist upon is the real presence of the past and the need for communion with it if transformation is to occur. The first of these scenes occurs, of course, in Chapter I, when the three artists detect Donatello's striking resemblance to the statue and name him the "very Faun of Praxiteles." In Chapter VII Hilda is startled to observe that Miriam's expression has become almost exactly that of Beatrice Cenci. The corpse of the dead Capuchin, with the blood oozing from its nostrils, assumes the likeness of all evil for Miriam in Chapter XXI. It symbolizes "the deadly iteration with which she was doomed to behold the image of her crime reflected back upon her in a thousand ways" (VI,

222). By this time Donatello has assumed a similar burden from the past, and his new awareness of its weight is typified in Chapter XXVIII when he takes up the alabaster skull of his ancestor and explains its meaning to Kenyon. Having done penance, Miriam and Donatello find their union blessed at "high noon" in Chapter XXXV, when the statue of Pope Julius seems to become "endowed with spiritual life." It is now Hilda's turn to recognize the bond, and in Chapter XLII she realizes for the first time the harshness of her earlier attitude toward Miriam. Now she is able to see the resemblance between herself and her former friend, and she makes what amounts to a penitential journey to the Palazzo Cenci, haunted by the "lovely shade of Beatrice."

The final "incarnation" takes place during the magnificent carnival scene of Chapter XLIX. Though Kenyon has been intellectually aware of the past, he has cherished a spiritual love for Hilda that has insulated him from the shocks of vital experience; he has resisted any real involvement with Miriam's trouble; and he has retreated from her suggested analogy between their story and the Fall of man. Now, in spite of himself, he becomes a part of the carnival. He finds his Hilda only after an exaggerated re-enactment of the Fall of man. A giant Eve, a female figure "seven feet tall," singles out the sculptor and makes "a ponderous assault on his heart." Failing in her first attempts, she shoots him in the heart with a popgun, "covering Kenyon with a cloud of lime-dust" (VI, 504). This affair is "like a feverish dream," a surrealistic version of Adam's reduction to human clay, but it qualifies Kenyon for union with the multifoliate rosebud, the spirit incarnate in Hilda.

As the characters in the book are gradually driven toward recognition of their resemblance to figures in timeless myth, the reader's insight simultaneously deepens to perceive the

HAWTHORNE'S TRAGIC VISION

relation of *The Marble Faun* to the literary tradition. Miriam is linked not only with Beatrice Cenci and Cleopatra but also with Eve, the Biblical Miriam, Jael, Judith, and Rachel. Donatello (Hawthorne seems to have given him this name because he recognized the Italian sculptor as an authentic primitive)[2] is linked with Adam before the Fall and with Cain after his crime. The pure innocence of Hilda has its historic counterparts in the Virgin Mary and in the saint whose name she shares (VI, 71).

As might be expected, echoes of Milton reverberate throughout the book. In the sculptor's studio Miriam discovers the "grand, calm head" of the great Puritan poet, a figure that could have been shaped only through "long perusal and deep love" of *Paradise Lost* and Milton's other poems. Surely we should take this as Hawthorne's own tribute to one who had preceded him in probing deep into man's universal nature. Immediately behind Miriam and Donatello stand the eternal woman and man in Milton's story of the Fall: the woman's yearning for further knowledge, her effort to achieve increased efficiency through division of labor— her desire, in short, to "know" the man; the man's initial unity with nature, his impassioned longing for a mate, and his "glorious trial of exceeding love" as he joins Eve in sin. The last four books of *Paradise Lost* remain the best introduction to Hawthorne.

The links with Shakespeare are less obvious but almost as important. The model, Miriam, Donatello, and Hilda are haunted by an indelible bloodstain that reminds us of Lady Macbeth's tortured efforts to cleanse her hands. In dealing with the contagiousness of evil, Hawthorne may have called to mind the dank, graveyard atmosphere of *Hamlet*, where the dram of evil infests all the noble substance of mankind.

[2] See Hawthorne's reference to Donatello (X,345).

The Transfiguration of Figures: The Marble Faun

There is something rotten in Rome as in Denmark; the skulls of the Capuchins and the corpse of Brother Antonio are reminiscent of Yorick and of Polonius at supper. "To Kenyon's morbid view, there appeared to be a contagious element rising foglike from the ancient depravity of Rome, and brooding over the dead and half-rotten city" (VI, 468). The impact of this atmosphere on the sculptor faintly resembles Hamlet's second and fourth soliloquies: "I am sluggish," Kenyon mutters; "a weak, nerveless fool, devoid of energy and promptitude." It takes all his energy to fling aside this mood of "morbid hesitation."

But Kenyon is not Prince Hamlet, nor was he meant to be. He is an attendant, an adviser, full of high sentence, and at times almost the Fool. Thus, as Matthiessen has observed, Hawthorne looks backward to Milton and forward to Eliot,[3] and not so much to Prufrock as to the *Four Quartets.* For *The Marble Faun* is concerned with the ways in which nature and spirit, innocence and evil, time and eternity may be conquered and reconciled in a moment of incarnation. Eliot's dove and rose are, of course, far removed from Hawthorne's, but the central experience is much the same. Eliot links spiritual conversion with poetry and music; Hawthorne unites it with sculpture and romance.

In *The Marble Faun,* the parallel between sculpture and life is introduced in the title, established in the first paragraph, and maintained throughout the book. The process of transfiguration is as central in art as it is in life. The three stages of sculpture—clay, plaster cast, and marble—are, as we have already noted, analogous to life, death, and resurrection. Hawthorne begins by describing the marble statues in the sculpture room at the Capitol, "shining in the un-

[3] Matthiessen discusses different parallels but comes to the same conclusion. *American Renaissance,* pp. 351–68.

diminished majesty and beauty of their ideal life," but at the
same time "corroded by the damp earth." In the statue of a
child "clasping a dove to her bosom, but assaulted by a
snake" is prefigured the choice between "Innocence or Evil"
—a choice that will affect the lives of the four individuals
standing in the room.

The whole problem of evil, of reconciling "the incongruity
of Divine Omnipotence and outraged, suffering Humanity,"
is in fact summed up in Kenyon's natural comparison of God
to a sculptor who "held the new, imperfect earth in his hand,
and modelled it" (VI, 305). In creating the world, God was
subject to the limitations of his art form, the imperfect clay
in which he worked. Clay is, as Miriam says, earthy and human. Kenyon's clay model captures "all Cleopatra—fierce,
voluptuous, passionate, tender, wicked, terrible, and full of
poisonous and rapturous enchantment." His clay bust of
Donatello similarly expresses the mixture of good and evil
that characterizes human life. Flexible, warm, impure, the
intricate shape of clay seems "more interesting than even the
final marble, as being the intimate production of the sculptor himself, moulded throughout with his loving hands, and
nearest to his imagination and heart" (VI, 140).

The beauty and life of the clay model disappear in the
plaster cast. Imbued with mortality, it has no celestial hopes;
it has the rigidity of marble with none of its purity. The
skull in Donatello's room is carved "in gray alabaster, most
skillfully done to the death, with accurate imitation of the
teeth, the sutures, the empty eye-caverns, and the fragile
little bones of the nose." The corpse of the dead Capuchin
congeals into a ghastly waxen hardness that fits it into this
grisly category. Like the macabre skulls in the Capuchin
cemetery, the corpse seems a malevolent mockery of man's
hopes for a future life.

But out of the clay and the plaster emerges the pure, white, undecaying figure done in marble, which assumes a sacred character. "It insures immortality to whatever is wrought in it, and therefore makes it a religious obligation to commit no idea to its mighty guardianship, save such as may repay the marble for its faithful care, its incorruptible fidelity, by warming it with an ethereal life" (VI, 163). Yet though the marble should resolve the feverish activity of life into a cool repose—"a blessed change," as Miriam calls it— too often it appears rigid, harsh, and remote from human concerns. "You are as cold and pitiless as your own marble," she exclaims, as she detects Kenyon's reluctance to become entangled in her affairs.

With this basic resemblance between sculpture and moral growth established, we may now proceed to Hawthorne's distinction between sculpture and painting. Sculpture, as he views it in this book, is essentially a masculine art form. It freezes an image in space and has nothing temporal about it. "Flitting moments," Kenyon observes, "ought not to be incrusted with the eternal repose of marble" (VI, 31). A sculptural subject, therefore, ought to be in a "moral stand-still." Painting, on the other hand, is essentially feminine. "Your frozen art," Miriam gibes, "has nothing like the scope and freedom of Hilda's and mine. In painting there is no similar objection to the representation of brief snatches of time." Painting, she adds, is a warmer, more heartfelt medium.

The man, therefore, is a sculptor, while the two women are painters. But the fact that Hilda is a "copyist" requires further comment if we are to understand the initial artistic situation. To put it schematically, at the outset Donatello is nature, Hilda is spirit, and Miriam and Kenyon are the two working artists. Donatello, obviously, is the object: he is all matter, though a spiritual potential may be discerned. Hilda, as spirit, sees *sub specie aeternitatis*. She looks right through the surface of paintings to the central point or aim of the artist; she works religiously; but she can create nothing new. Donatello is the origin, Hilda the "end." To be converted into art, Donatello must "unearth"; Hilda must "earth-stain." Viewed from this perceptive, the crucial moment comes late in the book when Donatello unearths the earth-stained statue of Venus de' Medici—a statue that reminds Kenyon of his quest for Hilda.

Truly creative art, therefore, requires both penetrative insight and sympathetic investment. Without the humane clothing of a sympathetic imagination, penetrative insight is like rigorous Freudian literary criticism; it plumbs the surface, but it leaves us with a nude, or at its worst, with a skull. On Hilda's religious plane it results simply in a pure copy of an unchanging idea. But investment without insight produces mechanical superficial copies far inferior to Hilda's spiritual imitations. Transformation of material into art must ultimately remain a mystery, a miracle. Like human conversion, it is consummated in a moment of immediate apprehension that comes as a reward for intellectual discipline and sympathetic understanding. The final product, the "genial moment" in which the inner germ finds the perfection of its outward form, is not entirely preconceived. With both his Cleopatra and his bust of Donatello, Kenyon begins hopefully with his conscious intentions, lives through a period of despair, and finally achieves the vital expression "independent of his own will."

This, I take it, is the way in which Hawthorne transformed his own "blocks of material" taken from his notebooks. We have to remember, however, that the notebook passages themselves were not simply raw material, recorded

at random from Hawthorne's experience. Selected in the
first place because they might bear upon the theme of a
future romance, many of these passages were sufficiently
"worked up" so that they needed little alteration when
placed in the context of his book. Like the fragments of
Venus de' Medici, they assume a new life and light when
joined with "the whole figure." Hawthorne's comments on
nude statuary, for instance, seem merely naïve and provincial when read in the *French and Italian Notebooks.* But
when voiced by Miriam and Kenyon, they are illuminated by
"the whole figure" of the book. In a fallen world, the chaste
nudity of innocence must be clothed by time and tragedy
before conversion can occur.

The discussions of art can be fully understood only as part
of the book's thematic structure. Its action we have outlined
as an ever widening four-part circle, revolving about a threefold central experience. After rebelling against her destined
role as woman, Mirian discovers her bond with time and the
specter of guilt; Donatello becomes passionately entangled
with Miriam and her guilt; Hilda becomes involved (though
vicariously) with Miriam, Donatello, and their guilt; and
finally Kenyon (in an even more diluted mode) recognizes
his relation to Miriam, Donatello, Hilda, and the total burden
of humanity.

It is fitting that Miriam should be the major figure in the
first part of the book, for she potentially offers what Rome
does—"all time." A prototype of womanhood like Beatrice
Rappaccini, Hester, and Zenobia, she seems to contain all
races in her rich, mysterious origins. There is "an ambiguity
about this young lady": linked like Eve and Pandora to the
very model of evil, she also bears the seed of maturity and
benediction. She seems so large and bounteous in this archetypal role that it comes as a shock to read her assumed name:

"Miriam Schaeffer, artist in oils." Her studio in the castle, like the rooms of the other characters, is a projection of her inner traits; it is "the outward type of a poet's imagination." In it are two kinds of sketches that clearly reveal her ambiguity. One is a group of scriptural subjects, showing again and again the idea of "a woman acting the part of revengeful mischief towards man" (VI, 61); the other is a series of domestic scenes, representing the "earthly paradise" that results from "wedded affection" and the newborn child. Miriam intuitively knows what Zenobia was finally forced to recognize: that "woman must strike through her own heart to reach a human life." The two groups of sketches thus illustrate "the life that belongs to woman."

At the outset, however, Miriam has rebelled against this life. She pictures herself as a figure apart, and in all the accounts supplied of her immediate background the one common element is her attempt to break the bond. Her original "crime," however, cannot be washed away or painted over. We know that her mother died when Miriam was an infant and that a marriage unsuitable for the daughter but convenient for the family fortunes had been arranged. Miriam's fiancé had been her cousin, a man whose character "betrayed traits so evil, so treacherous, so vile, and yet so strangely subtle, as could only be accounted for by the insanity which often develops itself in old, close-kept races of men, when long unmixed with newer blood" (VI, 487). She revolted against her father, repudiating the marriage contract. Then followed the nameless crime (probably, judging from the parallel with Beatrice Cenci, the murder of her father). Though innocent of legal guilt, Miriam was emotionally implicated in the crime, since her cousin clearly was the criminal. It is he who reappears in the catacombs, a spectral personification of evil and guilt. The model knew Miriam as a young girl (VI, 116, 223); that he is her former fiancé and cousin is clearly implied when she observes in retrospect that he must have been a madman. "Insanity must have been mixed up with his original composition, and developed by those very acts of depravity which it suggested" (VI, 488).

Legally innocent but morally guilty, affianced to satanic evil, Miriam obviously bears more than casual resemblance to Eve after her first depravity. Her original crime, like Eve's, was rebellion against the father ("Miriam" originally meant "rebellion"). Like Hester and Zenobia, however, she is linked not only to guilt but also to the vessel of purification; she is potentially a second Eve (again her name is significant: "Mary," of course, derives from Greek "Mariam," Hebrew "Miryam). Hilda is Miriam's closest friend; they are like "sisters of the same blood," containing between them the essence of womanhood. But unlike Pearl, who is Hester's seed and effectively bruises the head of the serpent, Hilda does not function very well as a narrative embodiment of woman's redemptive qualities. We note the meaning of her separation from Miriam and their eventual reunion, but it is not dramatically convincing.

Miriam's efforts to expunge her guilt, to find "new hopes, new joys," can only lead to further extension of her Original Sin. Once the man has fixed his lot with her, he is, as Milton says, "certain to undergo like doom." Donatello, whose transformation appropriately occupies the central portion of the book, is first introduced as the ultimate of primitive innocence. Free to gambol in space, he "has nothing to do with time" (VI, 29). In his animal-like youth, he enjoys the peak of intuitive sympathy with all forms of life. In order to mature, he must be educated through the heart by Miriam. But he educates her as well. She needs the ritual of the romp through the Borghese Eden, a refreshment from the fountain

of simplicity in order to assume her proper role as woman.
When she asks why he follows her, he answers simply, "Because I love you." There is no other way to say it, and he
saves her from moving into a brittle existence where such
sentiments, if uttered at all, would be verbalized into something like, "Our emotional impulses are integrated, and we
show promise of attaining a moral and intellectual con-
tinuum." He saves her, in short, from the rigid refinement of
a Kenyon.

The first fruit of Donatello's "marriage" with Miriam is a
feeling of fiery intoxication distilled out of their mutual guilt.
In a passage reminiscent of the forest scene in *The Scarlet
Letter*, Miriam urges Donatello to fling the past behind him.
"Forget it! Cast it all behind you," she urges. "The deed has
done its office, and has no existence any more." But it soon
becomes apparent that the specter of guilt is not buried this
easily. Donatello, like the fallen Adam, now repels the woman. He returns to his parental home to make that agonizing
reappraisal of his own heritage which is one of the first consequences of the union between man and woman. He has
lost his unity with nature; Miriam has lost her friendship
with Hilda.

Like Dimmesdale, Donatello now finds it necessary to
avoid men's eyes; he contemplates turning inward to a monk-
ish cell; he is overwhelmed by an exaggerated sense of the
past. But he has developed a new dignity, so that his title,
the Count of Monte Beni, now seems a more appropriate
name. Here in his native land, he and Kenyon educate each
other, the sculptor attempting to clarify the Count's muddled
thoughts after his shock of recognition, and the Count im-
plicitly demonstrating to Kenyon the difference between
vital involvement with the past and mere intellectual apprehension of it. The whole process of moral growth reveals

itself to Kenyon from Donatello's tower, as he gazes out over the valley (VI, 297).

What made the valley look still wider was the two or three varieties of weather that were visible on its surface, all at the same instant of time. Here lay the quiet sunshine; there fell the great black patches of ominous shadow from the clouds; and behind them, like a giant of league-long strides, came hurrying the thunderstorm, which had already swept midway across the plain. In the rear of the approaching tempest, brightened forth again the sunny splendor, which its progress had darkened with so terrible a frown.

The Count's great danger now, as his guide points out, is that he will be hypnotized by the vision of evil. Like Vergil advising Dante in Canto XXX of the *Inferno,* Kenyon tells Donatello that "it was needful for you to pass through that dark valley, but it is infinitely dangerous to linger there too long; there is poison in the atmosphere, when we sit down and brood in it!" (VI, 315). Though he is a wise counselor, Kenyon prefers not to become too deeply involved himself. He watches the process of treading out the wine press; he sees the laborer's feet and garments dyed red as with blood; but he declines a sample of the Tuscan wine. "He had tried a similar draught . . . in years past, and was little inclined to make proof of it again; for he knew that it would be a sour and bitter juice, a wine of woe and tribulation, and that the more a man drinks of such liquor, the sorrier he is likely to be" (VI, 317).

Donatello emerges from the valley and finds blessing when he rejoins Miriam under the statue of Pope Julius. Kenyon's remarks on their reunion are pontifical—he is, in effect, speaking for the Pope—but they make their point (VI, 370):

Not for earthly bliss, but for mutual elevation, and encouragement towards a severe and painful life, you take each other's hands. And if, out of toil, sacrifice, prayer, penitence, and earnest effort towards right things, there comes, at length, a sombre and thoughtful happiness, taste it, and thank Heaven! So that you live not for it,—so that it be wayside flower, springing along a path that leads to higher ends,—it will be Heaven's gracious gift, and a token that it recognizes your union here below.

As the Faun, the original type of man, finds his soul and struggles with it "towards the light of heaven," the heavenly vision is brought down to earth. The incarnation of the Holy Spirit in the Dove is, as most readers have agreed, the most ineffective portion of the book. We do not boggle at the dove symbol in Eliot's *Four Quartets;* and we might accept Hilda in a medieval dream vision, but in fiction she is impossible. She needs to be either more adult or else a child, like Pearl, Ilbrahim, or little Joe in "Ethan Brand." If she must be pictured as an adult, Hilda ought to be an ideal who is merely glimpsed at the end. When Hawthorne brings her out of her tower and involves her in the streets of Rome, we expect her to be more human than she can possibly be if she is to retain her allegorical function as spiritual purity. "It is like flinging a block of marble up into the air, and, by some trick of enchantment, causing it to stick there. You feel that it ought to come down, and are dissatisfied that it does not obey the natural law." This is Kenyon's observation about the timeless repose of marble, but it fits the problem of Hilda perfectly. She is associated throughout with the purity of marble. Even the marble image of her hand—the birthmark, the earthy part of Hilda that is all Kenyon can grasp—assumes its share of her remote divinity. Hawthorne apparently expected the reader to sense her icy rigidity and yet to sympathize with her. Thus he is forced into the excessive sentiment of such statements as "Poor sufferer for another's sin."

The Transfiguration of Figures: The Marble Faun

Nevertheless, this portion of the book has its high points: the description of Sodoma's Christ, with its parallel to Hilda's utter isolation in her vicarious atonement; her reaction to St. Peter's Cathedral; and, above all, her confession to the priest. As she yearns for the relief of the confessional, she sees the inscription *'Pro Anglica Lingua.'* It is "the word in season"; it is Hilda's opportunity to become part of the time-burdened human race; and here, for once, she is "softened out of the chillness of her virgin pride." That Hawthorne intended her to be delicately transformed into a woman from this point onward is clear when Kenyon finds the Venus Donatello has already unearthed. "What a discovery is here," he says. "I seek for Hilda, and find a marble woman! Is the omen good or ill?" The fact that the Venus is "slightly corroded" should supply his answer. But Hilda's purity is never more apparent and never more repulsive than it is in the final scenes with Kenyon.

Part of this is Kenyon's fault. If he is more substantial than Miles Coverdale, he is also much more stuffy. Hawthorne undoubtedly intended to portray the rigidity of the refined intellectual, but surely he did not mean Kenyon to be as insufferable as the modern reader finds him. It is impossible to believe that the man of marble could create a vital statue of Cleopatra. We wonder with Miriam: "Where did you get that secret? You never found it in your gentle Hilda." Kenyon does become slightly more human when Hilda disappears and he wanders in his labyrinth, the streets of Rome. And even he is swept into the swirling movement of the magnificent Carnival scene, as the seven-foot Eve covers him with lime dust. But his final union with Hilda, which should presumably result from a full comprehension of the whole experience, actually amounts to a retreat from it.

Both Hilda and Kenyon, therefore, convince us of the loss

that occurs in refinement. Kenyon, who apparently but not convincingly has earlier suffered through a tragic experience, is now content to distill life in his art and in his Hilda, who has her refined sculptor and her religion, which, like her art, is borrowed. Both ultimately remain spectators of the central experience of the book: the wedding of ultimate innocence—Etruria and the living Faun—with all time and all evil—Miriam and Rome.

Thus we are returned to the problem that has provoked much discussion: Does Hawthorne accept or reject the idea of the Fortunate Fall? Miriam, it will be recalled, offers this summary of the Romance:

The story of the fall of man! Is it not repeated in our romance of Monte Beni? And may we follow the analogy yet further? Was that very sin,—into which Adam precipitated himself and all his race,—was it the destined means by which, over a long pathway of toil and sorrow, we are to attain a higher, brighter, and profounder happiness, than our lost birthright gave? Will not this idea account for the permitted existence of sin, as no other theory can?

Kenyon retreats from her speculation at the time but repeats it a little later for Hilda's consideration. She, in turn, shrinks from the heretical doctrine and convinces Kenyon that this creed makes a mockery of religion and morality. What, then, was Hawthorne's position?

Hyatt H. Waggoner, in the most recent and detailed discussion of this problem, points out the logical implications of the Fortunate Fall:[4]

Adam's sin, so the argument runs, was the necessary means to man's final salvation, for if he had not sinned, Christ would not have needed to come and we would not know our present hope

[4] Waggoner, *Hawthorne*, p. 219.

The Transfiguration of Figures: The Marble Faun

of glory. Just so, the reasoning was sometimes continued, each one of the elect repeats Adam's history, "sinning" for the greater glory of God and in his own salvation. However one takes it, then, it is at least clear that sin is only good in disguise. In the rather secularized version of the idea presented in *The Marble Faun,* it is a necessary part of our education, a stepping stone to higher things. It is of course an apparently logical deduction from this that man should welcome and perhaps positively seek sin in order to cooperate with Providence.

As his tone would indicate, Waggoner then concludes that "there is every reason to believe that such a line of reasoning seemed to Hawthorne, as it did to Hilda, to make a 'mockery' of religious doctrine and moral law."

Once he has taken this position, however, Waggoner is forced to make a distinction between the meaning Hawthorne "intended" and the one he "achieved." For almost every page of the book indicates that without sin and suffering, moral growth rarely, if ever, results. With the examples of Miriam and Donatello fresh in our minds, it is difficult to see how any other interpretation is possible. Donatello is plunged "into those dark caverns, into which all men must descend, if they would know anything beneath the superficial and illusive pleasures of existence. And when they emerge, though dazzled and blinded by the first glare of daylight, they take truer and sadder views of life forever afterwards." Every human life, if it ascends to truth or delves down to reality, must undergo a similar change" (VI, 302). This progression is presented historically, with the glimpse back into the Golden Age, "before mankind was burdened with sin and sorrow, and before pleasure had been darkened with those shadows that bring it into high relief, and make it happiness" (VI, 104). It is presented scenically, when Kenyon beholds the sunshine, the shadow, the tempest, and finally the sunny splendor (VI, 297). And, as we have already seen, it is presented dramatically.

How, then, can so acute a critic as Waggoner argue that Hawthorne did not intend this meaning? Surely Waggoner is right when he says that Hawthorne, with Hilda, would reject the "line of reasoning" that is implied in the phrase "the Fortunate Fall." But he is just as surely wrong in saying that the narrative embodiment of the idea of redemption through sin is confined to Miriam; that she runs away with the book so that the achieved meaning differs from the intended meaning. The point is that Hawthorne and Hilda reject Kenyon's argument precisely because it is a line of reasoning. Take the narrative element out of the Christian story; make a logical formula (the Fortunate Fall) of it; remove the temporal lag between Adam's sin and Christ's redemption and it becomes a frozen creed that is at best a paradox, at worst a mockery of true morality. We recall that one of the main points of *The Scarlet Letter* was that moral truth must be apprehended as a narrative, a parable, an allegory—not as a line of reasoning. This of course, is only another way of expressing what Christians mean when they speak of "living by Christ." It is what Hawthorne meant when he found theological libraries to be a "stupendous impertinence."

The foregoing discussion prompts a final caution. The Biblical allusions in Hawthorne's work should not tempt us into reading it as scripture or theology. The Biblical tongues of flame enabled the apostles to preach orthodoxy, but in *The Scarlet Letter* Hawthorne shaped his own interpretation of the passage in Acts as he also formed his own religion. In that book Dimmesdale is in the church, while Hester remains outside of it; and in *The Marble Faun* the only religious edifice large enough to hold the characters at the end is the Pantheon. Hawthorne's position, to use R. W. B. Lewis'

The Transfiguration of Figures: The Marble Faun

phrase, was an offbeat traditionalism. His emphasis was not so much upon God's grace as it was upon man's struggle to achieve it. And ultimately the only way to come at his "religion" is to return to the living letter of his romances.

In Hawthorne's view no automatic formula suffices for meeting problems of the spirit. In this imperfect world some rise by sin and some fall by virtue. "Sometimes the instruction comes without the sorrow," but Hawthorne is dubious about this possibility. "Oftener the sorrow teaches no lesson that abides with us" (VI, 302). Dimmesdale ascends as a consequence of his sin; Young Goodman Brown's dying hour is gloom. Like Dimmesdale, Donatello rises spiritually and intellectually, although his flesh is incarcerated; Ethan Brand plunges into the pit. In order to develop his full human potential, man must become fully involved with time yet retain his unique ability to stand aside from its fleeting onrush and contemplate the eternal. This is the tragic vision of Hawthorne's fiction.

Index

180

Index

182

Index

185

Index

Hawthorne, Sophia: 8, 10 (n. 5), 18, 65, 101
Heilman, Robert B.: 81
Hillard, George: 33

Investment: 7–8, 72–88, 99–100, 169–70, 176; *see also* Feminine values.

James, Henry (1843–1916), novelist: 59, 91–92, 141
Jason (*The Faerie Queene*): 70
Johnson, Dr. Samuel: 33
Jones, Howard Mumford: 21 (n. 1)

Keats, John: 64
Kepler, Johannes: 80

Lamarck, Jean Baptiste de (naturalist): 120, 122
Lathrop, George P.: 5, 93 (n. 5)
Lawrence, D. H.: 29, 90, 141, 156
Leavis, Q. D.: 52 (n. 5)
Lewis, R. W. B.: 14 (n. 6), 27 (n. 12), 85 (n. 5), 176
Locke, John: 23–24, 26, 32, 34
Lovejoy, Arthur O.: 21 (n. 1), 25
Lubbock, Percy: 151
Lussky, A. E.: 21 (n. 1)
Lyell, Charles: 120

MacNamara, Anne M.: 92
Mann, Thomas: 141, 153
Marks, Alfred H.: 135 (n. 9)
Masculine values: 3, 7–12, 54–55, 99–100; *see also* Speculation
Matthews, J. C.: 60 (n. 4)
Matthiessen, F. O.: 32 (n. 19), 77, 150–51, 163
Melville, Herman: 14, 17, 20–21, 29–32, 35, 46–47, 57, 72–73, 75, 100, 145
Mencken, Henry L.: 127
Metcalf, Eleanor M.: 136 (n. 10)
Miller, Perry: 22 (n. 2), 26 (n. 9), 26 (n. 11)

Index

DATE DUE

GAYLORD			PRINTED IN U.S.A.